ANTHOLOGY FOR
Music in Western Civilization

VOLUME A:
ANTIQUITY THROUGH THE RENAISSANCE

ANTHOLOGY FOR
Music in Western Civilization

VOLUME A:
ANTIQUITY THROUGH THE RENAISSANCE

ANTHOLOGY FOR
Music in Western Civilization

VOLUME A:
ANTIQUITY THROUGH THE RENAISSANCE

Timothy Roden

Ohio Wesleyan University

Craig Wright

Yale University

Bryan Simms

University of Southern California

SCHIRMER
CENGAGE Learning™

Australia • Brazil • Japan • Korea • Mexico • Singapore • Spain • United Kingdom • United States

SCHIRMER
CENGAGE Learning

**Anthology for Music in Western Civilization
Volume A: Antiquity Through the Renaissance**
Timothy Roden, Craig Wright, Bryan Simms

Publisher: Clark Baxter

Associate Development Editor: Julie Yardley

Editorial Assistant: Emily Perkins

Executive Technology Project Manager:
Matt Dorsey

Executive Marketing Manager:
Diane Wenckebach

Marketing Assistant: Marla Nasser

Marketing Communications Manager:
Patrick Rooney

Project Manager, Editorial Production:
Trudy Brown

Creative Director: Rob Hugel

Executive Art Director: Maria Epes

Print Buyer: Karen Hunt

Permissions Editor: Kiely Sisk

Production Service: Stratford Publishing
Services

Text and Cover Designer: Diane Beasley

Copy Editor: Carrie Crompton

Autographers: A-R Editions, Highland
Engraving, Dennis Dieterich, and Mark Burgess

Cover Image: Carlo Saraceni (1585–1620), *Saint
Cecilia*. Galleria Nazionale d'Arte Antica, Rome,
Italy. Scala/Art Resource, NY.

Compositor: Stratford Publishing Services

For product information and technology assistance, contact us at
Cengage Learning Customer & Sales Support, 1-800-354-9706
For permission to use material from this text or product, submit all requests online at **cengage.com/permissions**
Further permissions questions can be emailed to
permissionrequest@cengage.com

Library of Congress Control Number: 2005925311

ISBN-10: 0-495-00879-6
ISBN-13: 978-0-495-00879-8

Schirmer
25 Thomson Place
Boston, MA 02210
USA

Cengage Learning is a leading provider of customized learning solutions with office locations around the globe, including Singapore, the United Kingdom, Australia, Mexico, Brazil and Japan. Locate your local office at:
international.cengage.com/region

Cengage Learning products are represented in Canada by Nelson Education, Ltd.

For your course and learning solutions, visit **academic.cengage.com**
Purchase any of our products at your local college store or at our preferred online store **www.ichapters.com**

Printed in Canada
3 4 5 6 7 8 11 10 09

CONTENTS

Part II
THE LATE MIDDLE AGES AND EARLY RENAISSANCE

 Part IV

BAROQUE MUSIC

COMPOSERS AND TITLES

PREFACE

$\mathcal{T}$he anthology that accompanies *Music in Western Civilization* provides students with study scores of representative compositions discussed in the text. By its very nature, an anthology must be selective, excluding some wonderful compositions while incorporating a few obscure ones. These lesser-known compositions uniquely demonstrate a specific aspect of the intersection of music with cultural expression. Whenever possible, however, it has been the intention of the authors to use famous works to ensure that students are familiar with the icons of Western music. It is important that students not simply recognize these masterpieces as sound bites heard in modern mass media, but that they have the opportunity to consider what has contributed to the enduring value of these works of sonic art.

To facilitate the study of each composition, the authors have provided introductions that offer further information about musical structure and historical background for each work. Absorbing all the facts mentioned in the text, anthology, and workbook can quickly become a daunting task for students. One highly recommended way to learn this mass of material is not by attacking the prose with a highlighter, but by transcribing the information about a composition's form, themes, and even specific chords into the score itself. Then, each time students follow the music (hopefully while listening to the CDs), they are reminded of the composition's most salient features, and begin to associate facts with musical sound.

Even the most cursory glance at a music library's catalog of scores will show that numerous editions are available for many works that appear in this anthology. Students (and instructors) may well wonder what criteria were used to select the scores that appear in this volume. We tried to achieve a balance between quality and cost by using scholarly editions that are in the public domain whenever possible. This was done in order to keep the price of the anthology as low as possible for college students. Further, as a special courtesy to students, many publishers and scholars made their editions available at a reduced rate. In a number of instances, piano/vocal editions were used to reduce space, and thereby allow for the inclusion of more compositions. Instructors may prefer a different version of a work from the one included in the anthology, which can provide an opportunity to discuss how editorial principles and practices have evolved over time.

Unless otherwise noted, the authors have provided translations of vocal music. Most Biblical texts are based on *The Holy Bible, translated from the Latin Vulgate and diligently compared with the Hebrew, Greek, and other editions in divers languages* (Philadelphia: John Murphy, 1914). Students may find the numbering of the psalms confusing because the Vulgate reduces the number of many psalms by one from the numbering system used in the King James and other Protestant editions of the Bible. For example, the well-known Twenty-third Psalm is the twenty-second in the Vulgate. Translations of the Mass Ordinary are based on the *Book of Common Prayer* (Boston: Parish Choir, 1899). With the exception of translations that are cited or located within the score, all other translations are by the authors.

This anthology would not have made it to press without the unstinting efforts of many individuals, and it is my pleasure to express my appreciation. It has been a privilege to work with Craig Wright and Bryan Simms. Their drafts and observations of the introductions as well as their generous expenditure of time and unfailing courtesy have made the compilation of the anthology a satisfying endeavor. Several scholars graciously allowed us to use their editions in this anthology: Alexander Blachly (Cordier), Daniel Heartz (Sermisy), Michael Holmes (Merulo), Valerie McIntosh (Jacquet de la Guerre), and Jonathan Zalben (Landini). Professor Heartz's transcription is a classic; the editions by the other scholars in the list represent some of the most recent musical research, and a few are published here for the first time. We are grateful for their contributions.

Without the help of libraries throughout the United States, this anthology would not have been possible. A few libraries were particularly generous in making their collections available for our use. In particular, I wish to thank Faith Hoffman and Deborah Campana of the Oberlin College Conservatory of Music Library, Barry Zaslow from Miami (Ohio) University Music Library, and Julie Niemeyer from Yale University Library. Without the help of Marsha Zavar (Interlibrary Loan, Ohio Wesleyan University), my sanity would have departed long ago for regions unknown. She spent many hours on the Internet and telephone helping to locate rare scores and microfilms, and urging various libraries to expedite their interlibrary loan process.

Our copyeditor, Carrie Crompton, caught countless inconsistencies and made numerous suggestions that improved the text immeasurably. Many music engravers (A-R Editions, Highland Engraving, Dennis Dieterich, and Mark Burgess) reset old scores into digital format, and their efforts will make reading the music much easier. Nancy Crompton of Stratford Publishing Services kept all the various drafts under control and brought what became a vortex of swirling papers to completion. I thank the publisher, Clark Baxter, for the opportunity to participate in this project, and the associate development editor, Julie Yardley, for guiding me through the process. On the editorial staff, Sue Gleason and Abbie Baxter also provided valuable advice. The assistance of Trudy Brown, senior production project manager; Diane Wenckebach, executive marketing manager; and Emily Perkins, editorial assistant, is greatly appreciated.

Closer to home, I thank Ohio Wesleyan University for its liberal support of this project. The provost granted a reduced teaching assignment, the academic dean provided funds for computer hardware and software, a TEW grant provided for travel and the acquisition of material, and the music department generously supported the project by allowing thousands of photocopies to be made on their machine (and budget). Without the patience and enduring support of my wife and sons, to whom I owe a really nice vacation, I would not have been able to complete my work on this anthology.

—Timothy Roden
May 15, 2005

CREDITS

Chapter 1. **2:** No.1—Mathiesen, Thomas. *Apollo's Lyre: Greek Music and Music Theory in Antiquity and the Middle Ages*. Lincoln, NE: University of Nebraska Press, 1999, p. 117. **4:** No.2—Mathiesen, Thomas. *Apollo's Lyre: Greek Music and Music Theory in Antiquity and the Middle Ages*. Lincoln, NE: University of Nebraska Press, 1999, p. 149.

Chapter 3. **5:** No.3—*Tecum principium*. In *Antiphonale Monasticum*, ed. by the Benedictines of Solesmes. Tournai: Desclee, 1934, p. 245. **6:** *Dixit Dominus*. In *Liber Usualis*, ed. by the Benedictines of Solesmes. Tournai: Desclee, 1962, p. 128. **7:** No. 4—*Liber Usualis*, ed. by the Benedictines of Solesmes. Tournai: Desclee, 1962, p. 365. **8:** No. 5—*Liber Usualis*, ed. by the Benedictines of Solesmes. Tournai: Desclee, 1962, p. 408. **9:** No. 6—*Liber Usualis*, ed. by the Benedictines of Solesmes. Tournai: Desclee, 1962, p. 29. **10:** No. 7—*Liber Usualis*, ed. by the Benedictines of Solesmes. Tournai: Desclee, 1962, pp. 16–18. **12:** No. 8—*Liber Usualis*, ed. by the Benedictines of Solesmes. Tournai: Desclee, 1962, p. 409. **13:** No. 9—*Liber Usualis*, ed. by the Benedictines of Solesmes. Tournai: Desclee, 1962, pp. 409–410.

Chapter 5. **14:** No. 10—*Hodie cantandus est nobis*. In Reier, Ellen Jane. "The Introit Trope Repertory at Nevers: MSS Paris B.N. LAT. 9449 and Paris B.N. LAT. 1235." University of California, Berkeley: Ph.D. diss., 1981, III: 30–31. **17:** No. 11—Courtesy of author Craig Wright. **19:** No. 12—*Liber Usualis*, ed. by the Benedictines of Solesmes. Tournai: Desclee, 1962, pp. 1810–1813. **24:** No. 13—Courtesy of author Timothy Roden. **26:** No. 14—Courtesy of author Timothy Roden.

Chapter 6. **28:** No. 15—Courtesy of author Timothy Roden. **30:** No. 16—Van der Werf, Hendrik. *The Chanson of the troubadours and trouvères: A study of the melodies and their relation to the poems*. Utrecht, The Netherlands: A. Oosthoek's Uitgeversmaatschappij NV, 1972, pp. 91–95. **32:** No. 17—Reprinted by permission of the publisher from *The Historical of Music-Volume I: Oriental, Medieval, and Renaissance Music*, edited by Archilbald T. Davison and Willi Apel, p. 16, Cambridge, Mass: Harvard University Press. Copyright 1946, 1949 by the President and Fellows of Harvard College.

Chapter 7. **34:** No. 18—Reprinted by permission of the publisher from *The Historical of Music—Volume I: Oriental, Medieval, and Renaissance Music*, edited by Archilbald T. Davison and Willi Apel, p. 23, Cambridge, Mass: Harvard University Press. Copyright 1946, 1949 by the President and Fellows of Harvard College. **37:** No. 19—Lopez-Calo, Jose. *La Musica Medieval en Galicia*. La Coruña, Spain: Fundacion Pedro Barrie de la Maza, Conde de Fenosa, 1982, pp. 46, 138.

Chapter 8. **39:** No. 20—*Le Magnus Liber Organi de Notre-Dame de Paris. Vol. III: Les Organa à Deus Voix pour la Messe (de Noël à la Fête de Saint-Pierre et Saint-Paul) du Manuscrit de Florence*, Bibliotecka Medicea-Laurenziana, Plut. 29.1. Ed. by Mark Everist. Les Remparts, Monaco: Éditions de L'Oiseau-Lyre S.A.M., 2001, pp. 1–14. **47:** No. 21—*Le Magnus Liber Organi de Notre-Dame de Paris. Vol. I: Les Quadrupla et Tripla de Paris*. Ed. by Edward H. Roesner. Les Remparts, Monaco: Éditions de L'Oiseau-Lyre S.A.M., 1993, pp. 1–14.

Chapter 9. **62:** No. 22—*Notre-Dame and Related Conductus. Part 9. Three-Part Conductus in Related Sources*. Ed. by Gordon Anderson. Henryville: Institute of Mediæval Music, 1986, p. 2. **64:** No. 23—*Notre-Dame and Related Conductus. Part 1. Four- and Three-Part Conductus in the Central Sources*. Ed. by Gordon Anderson. Henryville: Institute of Mediæval Music, 1986, pp. 50–52. **68:** No. 24a—*Le Magnus Liber Organi de Notre-Dame de Paris. Vol. V: Les Clausules a Deus Voix du Manuscrit de Florence*, Biblioteca Medicea-Laurenziana, Pluteus 29.1, Fascicule V. Ed. by Rebecca A. Baltzer. Les Remparts, Monaco: Éditions de L'Oiseau-Lyre S.A.M., 1995, pp. 105–105. **69:** No. 24b—"O quam sancta, quam benigna/ET GAUDEBIT," in Gordon Anderson, ed., *The Las Huelgas Manuscript, vol. 2: Motetti et Conductus, Corpus mensurabilis musicae 79-2.* (American Institute of Musicology, 1982). Reprinted with permission. **71:** No. 24c—"El mois d'avril/O quam sancta/Et gaudebit" is published in *The Montpellier Codex. Part II: Fascicles 3, 4, and 5*, edited by Hans Tischler, *Recent Researchers in the Music of the Middle Ages and Early Renaissance*, vols. 4 and 5 (Madison, WI: A-R Editions, 1978). Used with permission. **76:** No. 25—"On parole/A Paris/Frese nouvele" is published in *The Montpellier Codex. Part III: Fascicles 6, 7, and 8*, edited by Hans Tischler, *Recent Researchers in the Music of the Middle Ages and Early Renaissance*, vols. 4 and 5 (Madison, WI: A-R Editions, 1978). Used with permission.

Chapter 11. **79–80:** No. 27—*Quare Fremuerunt*. In *Polyphonic Music of the Fourteenth-Century. Vol. I. The Roman de Fauvel, The Works of Philippe de Vitry, French Cycles of the Ordinarium Missae*. Ed. by Leo Schrade. Les Remparts, Monaco: Éditions de L'Oiseau-Lyre, 1956, p. 4. **82:** No. 28—*Garrit Gallus/In nova fert/Neuma*. In *Polyphonic Music of the Fourteenth-Century. Vol. I. The Roman de Fauvel, The Works of Philippe de Vitry, French Cycles of the Ordinarium Missae*. Ed. by Leo Schrade. Les Remparts, Monaco: Éditions de L'Oiseau-Lyre, 1956, pp. 68–70. **87:** No. 29—McGee, Timothy J., *Medieval Instrumental Dances*. Bloomington: Indiana University Press, 1989, p. 64. **89:** No. 30—McGee, Timothy J., *Medieval Instrumental Dances*. Bloomington: Indiana University Press, 1989, pp. 131–132.

Chapter 12. **97:** No. 31—Guillaume de Machaut. *Oeuvres Complètes*. Vol. III. Ed. by Leo Schrade. Les Remparts, Monaco: Éditions de L'Oiseau-Lyre S.A.M., 1977, pp. 29–31. **101:** No. 32—Guillaume de Machaut. *Oeuvres Complètes*. Vol. IV. Ed. by Leo Schrade. Les Remparts, Monaco: Éditions de L'Oiseau-Lyre S.A.M., 1977, pp. 45–46. **103:** No. 33—Guillaume de Machaut. *Oeuvres Complètes*. Vol. V. Ed. by Leo Schrade. Les Remparts, Monaco: Éditions de L'Oiseau-Lyre S.A.M., 1977, p. 4. **105:** No. 34—Guillaume de Machaut. *Oeuvres Complètes*. Vol. III. Ed. by Leo Schrade. Les Remparts, Monaco: Éditions de L'Oiseau-Lyre S.A.M., 1977, pp. 1–4.

VIII. Ed. by John Stevens. London: Stainer & Bell, 1962, pp. 10–11. **280:** No. 72—Courtesy of author Timothy Roden. **284:** No. 73—Byrd, William. O Lord, make thy servant, Elizabeth. In *The Byrd Edition*. *Vol. 11. The English Anthems*. Ed. by Craig Monson. London: Stainer & Bell, 1983, pp. 51–56.

Chapter 27. 290: No. 74—Goe from my window. In *The Fitzwilliam Virginal Book*. *Vol. I*. Ed. by J. A. Fuller Maitland and W. Barclay Squire. Leipzig: Breitkopf & Härtel, [1899], pp. 42–46. **296:** No. 75—Weelkes, Thomas. As Vesta Was Descending. In *The English Madrigal School*. *Vol. XXXII. Madrigals: The Triumphs of Oriana to 5 and 6 voices. Composed by Divers several Authors*. Published by Thomas Morley in 1601. London: Stainer & Bell, 1923, 175–188. **310:** No. 76—Dowland, John. Flow My Tears. In *The English Lute Songs*. *Series I. Vols. 5 & 6. John Dowland: Second Book of Songs (1600)*. Rev. ed. by Thurston Dart. London: Stainer & Bell, 1968, pp. 4–6.

Chapter 28. 314: No. 77—Moro, lasso. In *Gesualdo di Venosa: Sämtliche Madrigale für Fünf Stimmen*. *Vol. 6*. Ed. by Wilhelm Weismann. Hamburg: Ugrino Verlag, 1957, pp. 74–77. **319:** No. 78—Cruda Amarilli. In *Tutte le Opere di Claudio Monteverdi*. *Vol. 5. Il Quinto Libro de Madrigali*. Ed. by Francesco Malipiero. N.p.: Nel Vittoriale Degli Italiani, 1927, pp. 1–4.

Chapter 30. 326: No. 79—"Funeste piagge" (excerpt from Jacopo Peri's *Euridice*, scene 5), is published in *Jacopo Peri: Euridice: An Opera in One Act, Five Scenes*, edited by Howard Mayer Brow, *Recent Researches in the Music of the Baroque Era*, vol. 36–37 (Madison, WI: A-R Editions, Inc., 1981.) Used with permission. **329:** No. 80—"Filli, mirando il cielo" by Giulio Caccini is published in *Giulio Caccini: Le nuove musiche*, edited by H. Wiley Hitchcock, *Recent Researces in the Music of the Baroque Era*, vol. 9 (Madison: WI: A-R Editions, Inc., 1970). Used with permission. **333:** No. 81—*Tutte le Opere di Claudio Monteverdi*. *Vol. 11. L'Orfeo, Lamento d'Ariana, Musice de Alcuni*. Ed. by Francesco Malipiero. N.p.: Nel Vittoriale Degli Italiani, 1929, pp. 1–2, 62-64, 83-90. **346:** No. 82—*Tutte le Opere di Claudio Monteverdi*. *Vol. 13. L'Incoronazione di Poppea*. Ed. by Francesco Malipiero. N.p.: Nel Vittoriale Degli Italiani, 1931, pp. 246–250.

Chapter 31. 352: No. 83—Gabrieli, Giovanni, "In Ecclesiis," in Richard Charteris, ed., *Opera Omnia*, vol. 5: Motets in 'Sacrae Symphoniae' (Venice, 1615) III, *Corpus mensurabilis musicae*, 12-5. (American Institute of Musicology, 1996). Reprinted with permission. **377:** No. 84—Hor ch' el Ciel e la Terra. In *Tutte le Opere di Claudio Monteverdi*. *Vol. 8. Madrigali Guerrieri, et Amorosi*. Ed. by Francesco Malipiero. N.p.: Nel Vittoriale Degli Italiani, 1929, pp. 39–56. **395:** No. 85—*14 Arien qus opus II (1651) für Sopran oder Tenor und Basso continuo*. Ed. by Richard Kolb. Kassel: Furore-Verlag, 1996, pp. 26–29. **402:** No. 86—Saul, Saul, was verfolgst du mich? In *Heinrich Schütz Sämmtliche Werke*. *Vol. 11. Symphoniae sacrae. Dritter Theil. Zweite Abtheilung*. Ed. by Philipp Spitta. Leipzig: Breitkopf & Härtel, 1891, pp. 99–108.

Chapter 32. 413: No. 87—Miserere. In *European Sacred Music*. Ed. by John Rutter and Clifford Bartlett. Oxford: Oxford University Press, 1996, pp. 2–21. **422:** No. 88—Missa Salisburgensis. In *Denkmäler der Tonkunst in Österreich. Jahrgang X. Band 20. O. Benevoli, Festmesse und Hymnus*. Vienna: Artaria, 1903, pp. 1–8. **439:** No. 89—Frescobaldi, Girolamo. *Ausgewählte Orgelwerke in Zwei Bänden*. *Vol. I. Fiori Musicali (1635)*. Ed. by Hermann Keller. Leipzig: C. F. Peters, 1943, pp. 1–4, 18–19. **444:** No. 90—Jephte. Ed. by Janet Beat. Borough Green, Sevenoaks, Kent: Novello, pp. 30–33. **454:** No. 91—*Cantata Pastorale per la Nativita di Nostro Signore Gesu Christo*. Ed. by Edward J. Dent. London: Oxford University Press, 1969.

Chapter 33. 460: No. 92—*Il Seicento Musicale Italiano*. Vol. 2. *Salomone Rossi: Sonate per sonar due viole da braccio & un chitarrone o altro strumento simile (dal III Libro)*. Ed. by Franco Piperno. Rome: Pro Musica Studium, 1980, pp. 34–43. **470:** No. 93—Corelli, Arcangelo. *Les Oeuvres de Arcangelo Corelli*. *Vol. II*. Ed. by J. Joachim & F. Chrysander. London: Augener, [1871], 195-199. **476:** No. 94—*Sinfonia in D (G.8)*, Giuseppe Torelli, edited by R. P. Block/E. H. Tarr. © 1976 Musica Rara, London. 2000 assigned to Breitkopf & Haertel, Wiesbaden. **485:** No. 95—*L'Estro Armonico, Op. 3*. Ed. by Christopher Hogwood. London: Ernst Eulenburg Ltd., 2002, pp. 172–195.

Chapter 34. 497: No. 96—Suite XII. In *Denkmäler der Tonkunst in Österreich. Jahrgang VI/2. Band 13. Johann Jakob Froberger, Clavierwerke II*. Vienna: Artaria, 1899, pp. 32–35. **501:** No. 97—Sonata XI, Auferstehung Jesu. In *Mysterien-Sonaten*. *Vol. III. Sonaten XI-XVI*. Ed. by Ernst Kubitschek. Vienna: Ludwig Doblinger (Bernard Herzmansky) KG, 2000, pp. 4–12. **511:** No. 98—Wie schön leuchtet der Morgenstern. In *Dietrich Buxtehudes Werke für Orgel*. *Vol. II*. Ed. by Philipp Spitta, rev. by Max Seiffert. Wiesbaden: Breitkopf & Härtel, 1904, pp. 73–77. **517:** No. 99—Wie schön leuchtet der Morgenstern. In *Denkmäler Deutscher Tonkunst. Vierter Jahrgang. Band I. Orgelkompositionen von Johann Pachelbel*. Leipzig: Breitkopf & Härtel, 1903, pp. 138–139. **520:** No. 100—Canon. In "Johann Pachelbel als Kammerkomponist." *Archiv für Musikwissenschaft I* (1918): 271–274.

Chapter 35. 536: No. 102—*Les Chaiers d'Elisabeth Jacquet de la Guerre*. Ed. by Catherine Zimmer. New York: OMI, n.d., pp. 43–46.

Chapter 36. 543: No. 103—"Tombeau de Madamoiselle Gaultier" by Denis Gaultier is published in *La Rhetorique des Dieux*, edited by David J. Buch, *Recent Researches in the Music of the Baroque Era*, vol. 62 (Madison, WI: A-R Editions, 1990). Used with permission. **545:** No. 104—*Oeuvres Complètes de François Couperin*. *Vol. II. Musique de clavecin I*. Ed. by Maurice Cauchie. Paris: Éditions de L'Oiseau Lyre chez Louise B. M. Dyer, 1932, pp. 107–110. **550:** No. 105—*Oeuvres Complètes de François Couperin*. *Vol. V. Musique de clavecin IV*. Ed. by Maurice Cauchie. Paris: Éditions de L'Oiseau Lyre chez Louise B. M. Dyer, 1932, pp. 64–65.

Chapter 37. 553: No. 106—Dido and Aeneas. In *The Works of Henry Purcell*. *Vol. 3. Dido and Aeneas*. Ed. by Margaret Laurie. London: Novello, 1979, pp. 94–96. **557:** No. 107—Come, Ye Sons of Art, Away. In *The Works of Henry Purcell*. *Vol. 24. Birthday Odes for Queen Mary, Part II*. Ed. by Bruce Wood. London: Novello, 1998, pp. 132–154. **573:** No. 108—The Queen's Funeral March and Canzona. In *The Works of Henry Purcell*. *Vol. 31. Fantazias and Miscellaneous Instrumental Music*. Rev. ed. by Michael Tilmouth, Alan Browning, and Peter Holman. London: Novello, 1990, pp. 97–98.

Chapter 38. 576: No. 109—Handel, George Frideric. Water Music. In *Georg Friedrich Händel's Werke*. *Vol. 47. Wassermusik, Feuerwerkmusik, Concerte und Doppelconcerte für grosses Orchester*. Ed. by Friedrich Chrysander. Leipzig: n.p., 1886, pp. 41–45. **583:** No. 110—Handel, George Frideric. Giulio Cesare. In *Georg Friedrich Händel's Werke*. *Vol. 68. Giulio Cesare*. Ed. by Friedrich Chrysander. Leipzig: n.p., 1875, pp. 52–58. **588:** No. 111—Handel, George Frideric. Messiah. In *Georg Friedrich Händel's Werke*. *Vol. 45. Messiah*. Ed. by Friedrich Chrysander. Leipzig: n.p., 1901.

Chapter 39. 620: No. 112—Orgelbüchlein. In *Johann Sebastian Bach's Werke*. *Vol. 25*. Leipzig: Breitkopf & Härtel, 1878. Reprint ed. Ann Arbor: J. W. Edwards, 1947, pp. 12–13. **622:** No. 113—Orgelbüchlein. In *Johann Sebastian Bach's Werke*. *Vol. 25*. Leipzig: Breitkopf & Härtel, 1878. Reprint ed. Ann Arbor: J. W. Edwards, 1947, p. 53. **624:** No. 114—Das Wohltemperirte Clavier. In *Johann Sebastian*

Bach's Werke. Vol. 14. Leipzig: Breitkopf & Härtel, 1866. Reprint ed. Ann Arbor: J. W. Edwards, 1947, pp. 6–9. **628:** No. 115—Brandenburg Concerto No. 5. In *Johann Sebastian Bach's Werke*. Vol. 19. Leipzig: Breitkopf & Härtel, 1871. Reprint ed. Ann Arbor: J. W. Edwards, 1947, pp. 127–148.

Chapter 40. **653:** No. 116—Wachet auf, ruft uns die Stimme. In *Johann Sebastian Bach's Werke*. Vol. 28. Leipzig: Breitkopf & Härtel, 1881. Reprint ed. Ann Arbor: J. W. Edwards, 1947. **704:** No. 117—*Messe in H-Moll*. Ed. by Christoph Wolff. Frankfurt: C. F. Peters, 1997, pp. 226–264.

ANTHOLOGY FOR
Music in Western Civilization

VOLUME I:
ANTIQUITY THROUGH THE BAROQUE

Part I

ANTIQUITY AND THE MIDDLE AGES

Chapter 1

Music in Ancient Greece

1

Euripides

Orestes, Stasimon Chorus (c408 B.C.E.)

Western culture has been enriched by the extraordinary artistic expression of the ancient Greeks. Their architecture, sculpture, literature, painting, and philosophy still influence our lives. Music, however, is an exception. While voluminous amounts of Greek theory have been preserved, very little ancient Greek music survives to the present day. Only about fifty musical artifacts exist, and most of those are fragmentary. One such scrap of music is a setting of an important chorus from the Greek tragedy *Orestes*, by the great playwright Euripides. The play, which scholars believe he wrote two years before his death in 406 B.C.E., might be called a sequel to the literary and poetic histories of the Trojan War. It tells the sad tale of Orestes, son of the great Greek warrior king Agamemnon, and of the tragic destruction of this once proud family following the Greek victory at Troy. Here the chorus—an important part in every Greek tragedy—steps forward to implore that Orestes be forgiven for murdering his mother, Clytemnestra.

Of all the ancient copies of the *Orestes*, only one fragment includes music for this chorus. The middle parts of seven consecutive lines of music are present on a fragment of papyrus a quarter the size of an ordinary paper napkin. The beginning and end of each line are missing. Thus, any recording of the Stasimon Chorus is a reconstruction in which the restorer fills in many missing pieces using educated guesswork. On this recording the notes are not played beginning to end. Rather, the phrases have been arranged to produce something of a free-form fantasia based on the original notation. In the score, brackets indicate those portions of text that are missing, but can be filled in from other sources. The original notation appears above the modern transcription. The various symbols, derived mainly from the Greek alphabet, form the Greek system of musical notation. They correspond to various pitches in the Greek Greater Perfect System. The octave species, or scale, employed here may be the Greek Phrygian (d, e, f, g, a, b, c', d') transposed to E (e, f♯, g, a, b, c♯', d', e'). But it seems to be inflected with the chromatic genus as well, which in this case produces a tetrachord represented by our modern pitches A, B♭, B, D. Needless to say, given so fragmentary a source and the distance in time between the fragment and the description of the Greek tonoi by theorists, any such analysis is extremely conjectural.

Listening to the recording, you will notice that the high G is not performed by the singer. The symbol that looks like a misshapen "Z" is believed to have indicated an instrumental flourish in the middle of the phrase. There are other symbols inserted between the text in the fifth and sixth lines, most probably noting instrumental passages. You will find the recording more intelligible if you play each line on the piano before listening to the selection.

Euripides
Orestes, Stasimon Chorus (c408 B.C.E.)
CD 1/1

[text uncertain]

What vengeful Demon thus with footstep dread,
Trampling the blood-polluted ground,
Sternly cruel joys to spread
Horror, rage, and madness round?
Woe, woe is me! In man's frail state
Nor height nor greatness firm abides.

Trans. by R. Potter, *The Plays of Euripides*, Everyman's
Library 63, ed. by Ernest Rhys (London: J. M. Dent, 1906), 207.

2

Seikilos
Skolion or Epitaph (first century C.E.)

The *Epitaph* of Seikilos dates from the first century C.E., more than four hundred years after the Stasimon Chorus (a longer period of time than separates our age from that of Bach). Although the poem is short, it contains four complete and consecutive lines of text. The music sits squarely in the Greek Phrygian mode (starting on E), without shifts from the diatonic genus to the chromatic genus.

Scholars knew nothing of this little poem until 1883. The text and music appear on a cylindrical tombstone. (A picture is posted on the Internet: www.seikilos.com.ar/Seikilos.htm). After its discovery in the old Ottoman Empire (now Turkey), the stone was placed in a museum in Smyrna, where it remained until the city was destroyed by fire in 1922. At some point after it was discovered and before it disappeared in the conflagration, the bottom of the column was ground down—obliterating the last line—so that it could stand upright and be used as a vase for flowers. After the fire, the tombstone was missing for thirty-five years, but amazingly reemerged in 1957 and is now part of an antiquities collection housed in the National Museum in Copenhagen.

As long as you live, shine
Grieve you not at all
Life is of brief duration
Time demands its end.

Adapted from Thomas J. Mathiesen, *Apollo's Lyre:
Greek Music and Music Theory in Antiquity* (Lincoln,
1999), p. 150.

Seikilos
Skolion or Epitaph (first century c.e.)
CD 1/2

Chapter

3

Music in the Monastery and Convent

3

Chants of Vespers
a. Antiphon, *Tecum principium*
b. Psalm, *Dixit Dominus*

What we today call Gregorian chant is a vast body of religious music for the Roman Catholic Church. It developed over many, many centuries, from the time of the earliest church fathers shortly after Christ until the Council of Trent (1545–1563), a reform-minded assembly that discouraged the creation of new chant and removed many chants that had been added to the Catholic liturgy over the centuries. Gregorian chant, sung in Latin, remained the official chant of the Roman Church until the Second Vatican Council (1962–1965), when vernacular languages and more informal musical practices were sanctioned within the church. The name "Gregorian" is, in truth, something of a misnomer. As far as is known, Pope Gregory I (590–605) composed no chants; he simply prescribed that certain chants be sung on specific days and seasons during the church year. Chant—also called plainsong and plain-chant—was composed long before Pope Gregory and long after.

The selection of chants contained in this anthology begins with music sung at the service of Vespers on Christmas Day. As with all of the canonical hours such as Vespers, the core of the music is a collection of psalms drawn from the Psalter. The first psalm for Vespers on Christmas Day is Psalm 109, *Dixit Dominus* (*My Lord said unto me*). It is chanted to a psalm tone that centers around a recitation pitch, here the pitch A. The psalm *Dixit Dominus* has eight verses. It is sung antiphonally, one verse by one half of the choir, the next by the other, alternating back and forth. At the end of the psalm comes the doxology, a standard formula in praise of the Trinity. Psalms at the canonical hours are preceded and followed by an antiphon, a relatively brief and generally neumatic chant. The antiphon here is *Tecum principium* (*With thee is the principality*), and its text offers a Christian introduction to the psalm, which originated among the Jews and is preserved in the Old Testament. Both antiphon and psalm are in the Dorian mode. Note that the antiphon seems to end with the letters "EUOUAE." This is a cue that tells the singers which psalm tone to use for *Dixit Dominus* and how to end that psalm. The letters stand for the vowels in the last phrase of the doxology: "saeculorum amen." The antiphon itself (and the entire antiphon-psalm-doxology-antiphon complex) actually ends on the pitch D at the end of "genui te."

Chants of Vespers
a. Antiphon, *Tecum principium*
CD 1/3

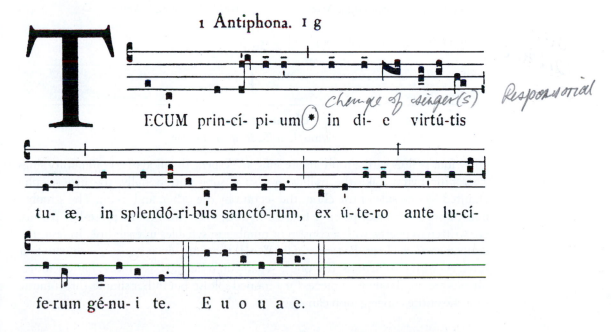

Antiphon

Tecum principium in die virtutis tuae,
in splendoribus sanctorum,
ex utero ante luciferum genui te.

With thee is the principality in the day of thy strength: in the brightness of the saints: from the womb before the day star I begot thee.

Chants of Vespers
b. Psalm, *Dixit Dominus*
CD 1/3

antiphonal
one line repeated throughout psalm

1. Di-xit Dóminus Dómino mé-   o : * Séde a *déxtris* mé-   is.

Psalm 109: Dixit Dominus

1	Dixit Dominus Domino meo:	The Lord said to my Lord:
	sede a dextris meis	Sit thou at my right hand:
2	Donec ponam inimicos tuos	Until I make thy enemies
	scabellum pedum tuorum.	thy footstool.
3	Virgam virtutis tuae emitte: Dominus	The Lord will send forth the sceptre of thy
	ex Sion:	power out of Sion:
	in medio inimicorum tuorum.	rule thou in the midst of thy enemies.
4	Tecum principium in die virtutis tuae	With thee is the principality in the day of thy
	in splendoribus sanctorum:	strength: in the brightness of the saints:
	ex utero ante luciferum genui te.	from the womb before the day star I begot
		thee.

Choirs 1 & 2 alternate verses

[Four additional verses follow]

9	Gloria Patri, et Filio,	Glory be to the Father, and to the Son,
	et Spiritui Sancto.	and to the Holy Ghost.
10	Sicut erat in principio, et nunc, et	As it was in the beginning, is now, and ever
	semper,	shall be,
	et in saecula saeculorum. **Amen.**	world without end. Amen.

Doxology both choirs

all for 2nd time

[Return to Antiphon *Tecum principium.*] *page 5*

4

Chants of Vespers
Hymn, Jesu, Redemptor omnium

After four psalms with antiphons are sung at Vespers, the monastic community sings a strophic hymn. Like the psalms, it also is sung antiphonally, the first strophe chanted by one side of the choir, the second by the other, and so on. The strophic musical setting is made possible because hymns, in contrast to the prose-like psalms, are written as poetry, with a consistent number of syllables in each line. In *Jesu, Redemptor omnium* (*Jesus, Redeemer of the World*) there are seven stanzas, each with four lines. As with most hymns, this one is syllabic in style and has a rather narrow range. Hymns are not flamboyant pieces for a trained soloist, but rather simple, direct music that the entire congregation can sing.

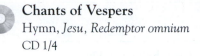

Chants of Vespers
Hymn, *Jesu, Redemptor omnium*
CD 1/4

between neumatic & syllabic
7 stanzas

8 syllables

1st & last line
repeat melodic line

Jesu, Redemptor omnium, Quem lucis ante originem, Parem paternae gloriae Pater supremus edidit.	Jesus, redeemer of the world, Who was the light before the beginning, The supreme Father begot An equal to his paternal glory.
Tu lumen et splendor Patris, Tu spes perennis omnium: Intende quas fundunt preces. Tui per orbem servuli.	You, light and splendor of the Father, You, eternal hope of all things: Hear the prayers of your people Throughout the world.
Memento, rerum Conditor, Nostri quod olim corporis, Sacrata ab alvo Virginis Nascendo, formam sumpseris.	Be mindful, creator of all things, That in the Virgin's sacred womb You were conceived and of her flesh, And born, did our human form assume.
Testatur hoc praesens dies, Currens per anni circulum. Quod solus e sinu Patris Mundi salus adveneris.	The present day affirms, A reminder throughout the year, That you alone from the Father's bosom Descended, savior of the world.
Hunc astra, tellus aequora, Hunc omne, quod caelo subest, Salutis auctorem novae Novo salutat cantico.	This, the stars, the earth, and the seas, The heavenly universe, Sound forth in a new song Of the creator of a new salvation.
Et nos, beata quos sacri Rigavit unda sanguinis, Natalis ob diem tui, Hymni tributum solvimus.	And we, too, were cleansed By a font of divine blood. Thus on this natal day of yours We offer hymns of tribute.
Jesu, tibi sit gloria, Qui natus es de Virgine, Cum Patre et almo Spiritu In sempiterna saecula. Amen.	Jesus, to you may glory be, You who are born of the Virgin, With the Father and the Holy Spirit, For now and forever. Amen.

5

Chants Beginning the Mass for Christmas Day
Introit, *Puer natus est nobis*

Mass is a unique religious service, usually celebrated in the morning, during which communion is taken. Mass chants fall into one of two general categories: those of the Proper of the Mass and those of the Ordinary. Proper chants are those setting a text tied to specific days of the year, such as the feast of St. Peter or Christmas Day. Ordinary chants are those setting a much more general text, such as the *Kyrie eleison* (*Lord, have mercy upon us*). The Mass begins with an Introit, a Proper chant that allowed the celebrating clergy to process to the altar singing a text appropriate to that day. The Introit *Puer natus est nobis* (*A boy is born to us*), for example, is sung only on Christmas morning. It consists of an antiphon ("Puer" down to "Angelus") followed by a single verse of Psalm 98 (beginning "Cantate Domino"), a cue to sing the doxology (beginning "Gloria Patri"), and, finally, a return to the antiphon. Thus, this Introit ends on the pitch G at the end of the word "Angelus."

Introit, *Puer natus est nobis*
CD 1/5

Puer natus est nobis,	A boy is born to us,
et filius datus est nobis:	and a Son is given to us;
cujus imperium super humerum ejus:	whose government is upon His shoulder;
et vocabitur nomen ejus,	and His name shall be called
magni consilii Angelus.	the Angel of great counsel.
Cantate Domino canticum novum:	Sing ye to the Lord a new song,
quia mirabilia fecit.	because He hath done wonderful things.
Gloria Patri, et Filio,	Glory be to the Father, and to the Son,
et Spiritui Sancto.	and to the Holy Ghost.
Sicut erat in principio, et nunc, et semper, et in	As it was in the beginning, is now, and ever shall be,
saecula saeculorum. **Amen.**	world without end. Amen.

6

Chants Beginning the Mass for Christmas Day
Kyrie, Omnipotens genitor

The Introit is followed by two chants of the Ordinary of the Mass, the melismatic *Kyrie* and the neumatic *Gloria*. These texts are general in tone and, as is true for the other parts of the Ordinary of the Mass (*Credo, Sanctus,* and *Agnus dei*), they are sung at almost every Mass throughout the church year. Ordinary chants are sung by the full choir, once a cantor or a celebrant has given the opening pitch. The *Kyrie* is the only portion of the Mass sung in Greek instead of Latin. This melody dates from the tenth century, as does the chant of the following *Gloria*. This *Kyrie*, like all *Kyrie* chants, involves a threefold repetition of the text that forms a petition for mercy. The first two petitions are stated three times to the same music; the third petition, however, concludes with a more elaborate version of the basic *Kyrie* melody. One unique aspect of this particular *Kyrie* is its ending; it does not conclude on the expected D final of the Dorian mode. In all other ways, however, this is a typical—and very beautiful—*Kyrie* melody.

 Kyrie, Omnipotens genitor
CD 1/6

Kyrie eleison.	Lord, have mercy upon us.
Christe eleison.	Christ, have mercy upon us.
Kyrie eleison.	Lord, have mercy upon us.

7

Chants Beginning the Mass for Christmas Day
Gloria No. 1

Unlike the *Kyrie*, the *Gloria* is a lengthy text that does not involve direct textual repetitions. Nonetheless, there is a prominent musical phrase at work here that moves up stepwise, G, A, to B. Sometimes it is brief, sometimes rather lengthy, depending upon the amount of text it must serve. Comparing the settings of "Adoramus te" with "Gratias agimus tibi" will show how flexible this phrase can be. Another phrase with a distinct leap upward of a fifth operates in a similar manner. This type of elaboration upon one or two prominent phrases is typical of the *Gloria* as a class of chant. As the opening line, "Glory to God in the highest," suggests, the *Gloria* incorporates a lengthy series of adulatory exclamations and celebrates the majesty of the Lord.

Gloria No. 1
CD1/7

unigéni-te   Jé-su Chríste.   Dó- mi-ne Dé- us,   Agnus

Dé- i, Fí- li- us Pá-tris. Qui tóllis peccá-ta múndi, mi-se-

ré-re nó- bis. Qui tóllis peccá-ta múndi,   súscipe depreca-

ti- ónem nóstram. Qui sédes ad déx-te-ram Pátris, mi-se-

ré-re nó- bis. Quóni- am tu só-lus sánctus. Tu sólus Dó-

minus. Tu só-lus Altíssimus, Jé-su Chríste.   Cum Sáncto

Spí-ri- tu,   in gló-ri- a Dé- i Pá-tris. A-   men.

Gloria in excelsis Deo	Glory to God in the highest,
Et in terra pax hominibus bonae voluntatis.	and on earth peace, goodwill towards men.
Laudamus te.	We praise Thee,
Benedicimus te.	we bless Thee,
Adoramus te.	we worship Thee,
Glorificamus te.	we glorify Thee,
Gratias agimus tibi propter magnam gloriam tuam.	we give thanks to Thee for Thy great glory.
Domine Deus Rex caelestis,	O Lord God, heavenly King,
Deus Pater omnipotens.	God the Father Almighty.
Domine Fili unigenite Jesu Christe.	O Lord, the only begotten Son, Jesus Christ.
Domine Deus, Agnus Dei, Filius Patris.	O Lord God, Lamb of God, Son of the Father.
Qui tollis peccata mundi,	Thou that takest away the sins of the world,
miserere nobis.	have mercy on us.
Qui tollis peccata mundi,	Thou that takest away the sins of the world,
suscipe deprecationem nostram.	receive our prayer.
Qui sedes ad dexteram Patris,	Thou that sittest at the right hand of God the Father,

miserere nobis.	have mercy on us.
Quoniam tu solus sanctus.	For Thou alone art holy,
Tu solus Dominus.	Thou alone art the Lord;
Tu solus Altissimus, Jesu Christe.	Thou alone, O Christ,
Cum Sancto Spiritu,	with the Holy Ghost, art most high
in gloria Dei Patris. Amen.	in the glory of God the Father. Amen.

8

Chants Beginning the Mass for Christmas Day
Gradual, *Viderunt omnes*

The succeeding Gradual, *Viderunt omnes*, and *Alleluia. Dies santificatus* are Proper chants that speak specifically to the events and religious meaning of Christmas. Both are responsorial chants—the full choir responds to a soloist who sings the verse. Moreover, both are highly melismatic and offer a soloist the opportunity to demonstrate unusual vocal skills in the musically difficult verse. In *Viderunt omnes* the verse, which is drawn from Psalm 97, begins with the text "Notum fecit Dominus." Notice the lengthy melisma on the word "Dominus" that offers the soloist a chance to shine as the phrase reaches up for a high F. This verse is typical of many Graduals in the Lydian mode in that it emphasizes the pitches A and C, using them to serve as something akin to recitation tones. After the verse, the respond should be repeated by the full choir, although today not all monastic and cathedral groups perform the repeat.

Gradual, *Viderunt omnes*
CD 1/8

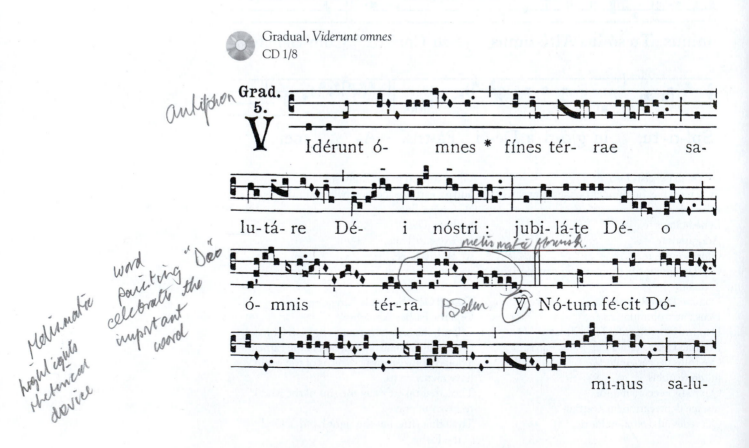

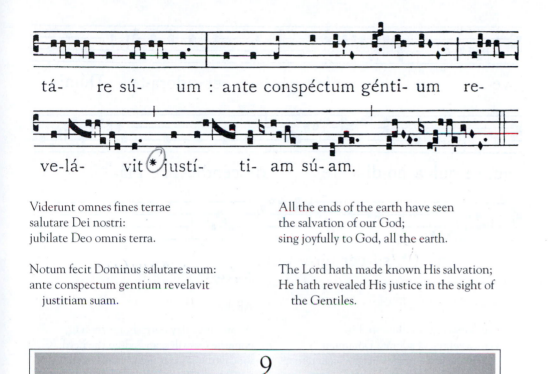

tá- re sú- um : ante conspéctum génti- um re-

ve-lá- vit justí- ti- am sú- am.

Viderunt omnes fines terrae	All the ends of the earth have seen
salutare Dei nostri:	the salvation of our God;
jubilate Deo omnis terra.	sing joyfully to God, all the earth.
Notum fecit Dominus salutare suum:	The Lord hath made known His salvation;
ante conspectum gentium revelavit	He hath revealed His justice in the sight of
justitiam suam.	the Gentiles.

9

Chants Beginning the Mass for Christmas Day
Alleluia, *Alleluia. Dies sanctificatus*

The Alleluia is sung during most of the liturgical year, except during the solemn penitential season of Lent. As its opening word suggests, this is a joyful chant, and the clerical community is given an opportunity to express its joy. It does so, in particular, with the extended melisma on the final "a," called the *jubilus*. Again, the Alleluia is a responsorial chant, so the verse is sung by a soloist and after it the full community responds with "Alleluia." Thus *Alleluia. Dies sanctificatus* concludes after the return of the respond, toward the end of the first system on the pitch D.

Alleluia, *Alleluia. Dies sanctificatus*
CD 1/9

Lle-lú-ia. *ij. Dí-*

es sancti- ficátus illúxit nó- bis :

Alleluia.

Dies sanctificatus illuxit nobis:
venite gentes, et adorate Dominum:
quia hodie descendit lux magna super terram.

Alleluia.

A sanctified day hath shone upon us;
come ye Gentiles, and adore the Lord;
for this day a great light hath descended
upon the earth.

Later Medieval Chant
Tropes, Sequences, and the Liturgical Drama of Hildegard of Bingen

10

Tuotilo of St. Gall
Introit trope, *Hodie cantandus est nobis* (c900)

A thousand years ago, this famous trope was used in the monastery of St. Gall to begin the Mass on Christmas morning. Serving as a preface to the Introit *Puer natus est nobis*, it can be interpreted as a conversation between the angels and shepherds described in the Christmas story.

There are three sections to this narrative: the announcement of the holy birth; the response (the translation divides this into two sentences); and the answer to the preceding question along with the transition into the Introit. Because of this dialogue, *Hodie cantandus est nobis* is a forerunner of the emerging liturgical drama (see no. 14). The different parts may possibly have been sung by separate soloists representing the angels and shepherds. The musical structure parallels the literary form, with musical cadences occurring on closing phrases of the text. The first two sections are clearly in the first, or Dorian, mode, but since the Introit is in the seventh (Mixolydian) mode, the third phrase has to effect a modulation, and so the final phrase of the trope concludes on G.

Tuotilo of St. Gall
Introit trope, *Hodie cantandus est nobis* (c900)
CD 1/10

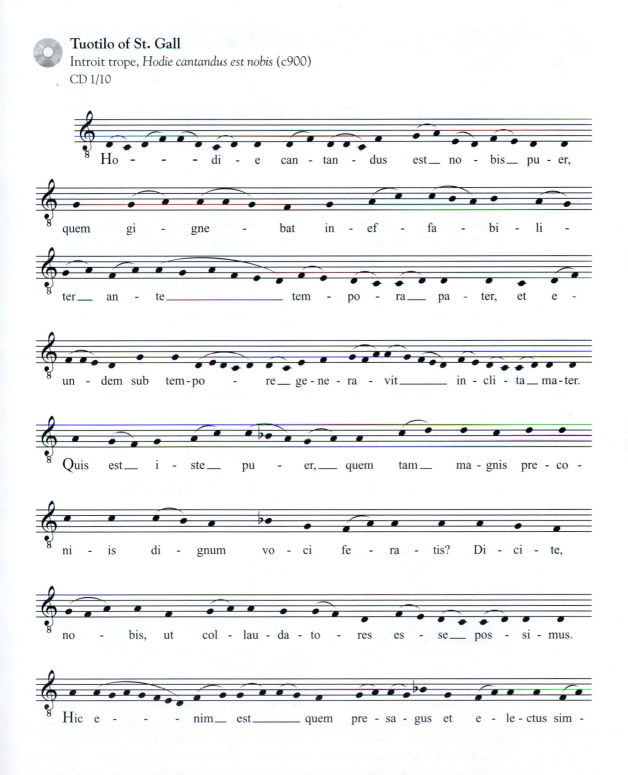

Ho - - - di - e can - tan - dus est— no - bis— pu - er,

quem gi - gne - bat in - ef - fa - bi - li -

ter— an - te— tem - po - ra— pa - ter, et e -

un - dem sub tem - po - re— ge - ne - ra - vit— in - cli - ta - ma - ter.

Quis est— i - ste— pu - er,— quem tam— ma - gnis pre - co -

ni - is di - gnum vo - ci fe - ra - tis? Di - ci - te,

no - bis, ut col - lau - da - to - res es - se— pos - si - mus.

Hic e - - - nim— est— quem pre - sa - gus et e - le - ctus sim -

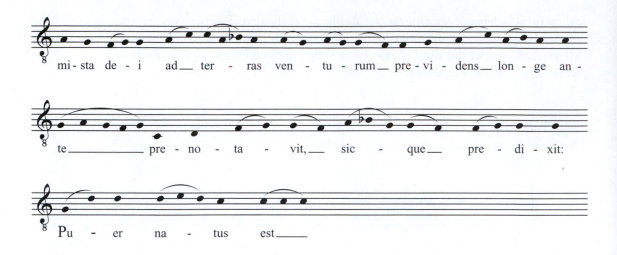

mi - sta de - i   ad ter - ras ven - tu - rum__ pre - vi - dens__ lon - ge an -

te_____ pre - no - ta - vit,__ sic - que__ pre - di - xit:

Pu - er na - tus est__

Hodie cantandus est nobis puer, quem gignebat
ineffabilter ante tempora pater,
et eundum sub tempore generavit inclita mater.

Quis est iste puer, quem tam magnis praeconiis
dignum voci feratis?

Dicite, nobis, ut collaudatores esse possimus.

Hic enim est quem praesagus et electus symmista
Dei ad terras venturum
praevidens longe ante praenotavit, sique praedixit:

[Introit:] Puer natus est nobis . . .

Today we sing of a child, begotten
ineffably, eternally, of the father
and born of this world, of the holy mother.

Who is this child, whom you say is
worthy of such great praise?

Tell us, so that we might all praise him joyfully.

For here is the child whom the chosen prophet
of God foretold
and said would come to earth long ago, predicting thus:

[Introit:] A boy is born to us . . .

*The Introit for High Mass on Christmas Day continues from this point; see no. 5, p. 8.

11

Tuotilo of St. Gall
Kyrie trope, *Omnipotens genitor* (c900)

Kyrie, Omnipotens genitor illustrates a second method of creating a trope. In *Hodie cantandus est nobis*, the music and text occur entirely before the beginning of the subsequent Introit, *Puer natus*. Singers could add or omit the trope without affecting the chant itself. *Omnipotens genitor* is different: the additional text exists within the melismatic passages of the chant itself. Instead of simply repeating the words "Kyrie" (Lord), "Christe" (Christ), and "Kyrie" for a total of nine statements, each invocation expands the text by adding devotional reflections on attributes of the Father, Son, and Holy Spirit.

While the text was eventually eliminated, the melody became a particular favorite. For centuries, composers selected this *Kyrie* for polyphonic elaboration (for an example, see no. 34, Machaut's *Messe de Nostre Dame*). It is still used in Roman Catholic liturgy today, appearing in the *Liber Usuális* and other liturgical books as *Kyrie IV*, with the subtitle *Cunctipotens* (an alternative spelling of *Omnipotens*) *genitor Deus*.

Tuotilo of St. Gall
Kyrie trope, Omnipotens genitor (c900)
CD 1/11

Om - ni - po - tens gen - i - tor De - us_____ om - nium
Fons et o - ri - go bo - ni pi - e_____ lux - que
Sal - vi - fi - cet pi - e - tas tu - a_____ nos bo -

cre - a - tor,_____ e - - - - - - le - i - son._____
pe - ren - nis,_____ e - - - - - - le - i - son._____
ne rec - tor,_____ e - - - - - - le - i - son._____

Chri - ste_____ De - i for - ma,_____ vir - tus pa - tris -
Chri - ste_____ pa - tris splen - dor,_____ or - bis lap - si
Ne tu - - - a dam - ne - mur_____ Je - su fac - tur -

que so - phi - a,_____ e - - - - le - i - son._____
re - pa - ra - tor,_____ e - - - - le - i - son._____
a be - ni - gne,_____ e - - - - le - i - son._____

Am - bor - um sac - rum spi - ra - men nex - us a - mor -
Pro - ce - dens fo - mes vi - tae, fons pu - ri - fi - cans

que,_____ e - - - - - - - le - i - son._____
nos,_____ e - - - - - - - le - i - son._____

Pur - ga - tor cul - pae, ve - niae lar - gi - tor op - ti -

me, _____ of - fen - sas de - le, san - cto nos mu - ne -

re re - ple, _____ e - - - - - - le - i - son. _____

Omnipotens genitor Deus, omnium creator, eleison.	Almighty father, God, creator of all things, have mercy.
Fons et origo boni pie luxque perennis, eleison.	Font of love, source of goodness, everlasting light, have mercy.
Salvificet pietas tua, nos bone rector, eleison.	May your love save us, good ruler, have mercy.
Christe Dei forma, virtus patrisque sophia, eleison.	Christ, form of God, virtue and wisdom of the Father, have mercy.
Christe patris splendor, orgis lapsi reparator, eleison.	Christ, splendor of the Father, redeemer of the fallen world, have mercy.
Ne tua damnemur Jesu factura benigne, eleison.	May your mercy prevent our damnation, mild Jesus, have mercy.
Amborum sacrum spiramen nexus amorque, eleison.	Holy Spirit, love, together with the Father and the Son, have mercy.
Procedens fomes vitae, fons purificans nos, eleison.	Life force infused, font of our purification, have mercy.
Purgator culpae, veriae largitor optime, offensas dele, sancto nos munere reple, eleison.	Cleanser of fault, all-generous imparter of pardon, blot out our offenses, fill us with holiness, have mercy.

12

Anonymous
Dies irae (c1250)

According to tradition, the authorship of this famous sequence is attributed to an Italian monk, Thomas of Celano (died c1250), who lived almost four centuries after Tuotilo and Notker Balbulus. Thomas was a close friend of St. Francis of Assisi and wrote two biographies of the saint; however, it is impossible to verify if he wrote either the text or music of *Dies irae*. The text of this sequence consists of nineteen stanzas. The first seventeen are uniform in poetic meter and rhyme: three eight-syllable lines with the same rhyme pattern (**AAA, BBB, CCC**, etc.). The last two stanzas are different. The eighteenth (which the music divides into two verses) has four lines and an **AABB** rhyme, while the final stanza has two unrhymed lines of seven syllables. It is believed that this final couplet was a later addition to the sequence. As is typical of sequences, the musical setting employs the double verse structure, in which pairs of stanzas are sung to the same music. This creates an **AABBCC** musical form for the first six stanzas. (Due to space limitations on the CD, it was necessary to abbreviate the recording of the *Dies irae*.)

The text has two themes: a terrifying depiction of Judgment Day and a plea for mercy. While later composers of requiems, especially Mozart, Berlioz, and Verdi, provided highly dramatic settings for this descriptive prayer, they did not use the chant. Beginning in the nineteenth century, other composers such as Liszt, Mussorgsky, and Saint-Saëns began to use the **A** theme of the *Dies irae* melody to convey images of death and demonic activity. It is this association that continues to resonate with the most force today, especially in the cinema.

Anonymous
Dies irae (c1250)
CD 1/12

Seq. 1.

DI- es írae, dí- es ílla, Sólvet saéclum in favílla :

Téste Dávid cum Sibýlla. Quántus trémor est futúrus,

Quando jú-dex est ventúrus, Cúncta stricte discussúrus!

Túba mí-rum spár-gens sónum Per sepúlcra regi- ónum,

Cóget ómnes ante thrónum. Mors stupé-bit et natú-

ra, Cum resúrget cre-a-túra, Judi-cán-ti responsúra.

Líber scríptus pro-fe-ré-tur,   In quo tó-tum continé-tur,

Unde múndus judi-cé-tur.   Júdex ergo cum sedébit,

Quídquid lá-tet apparébit :   Nil inúltum remanébit.

Quid sum mí-ser tunc dictúrus? Quem patró- num roga-tú-

rus? Cum vix jústus sit secúrus.   Rex treméndae ma-je-

stá-tis, Qui sal-vándos sálvas gra-tis,   Sálva me, fons pi- e-

tá-tis.   Recordá-re   Jé- su pí- e,   Quod sum cáusa tú-ae

ví-ae : Ne me pér-das   ílla dí- e. Quaérens me, se- dí-

sti lássus : Redemísti crúcem pássus : Tántus lá- bor non

sit cássus. Júste júdex ul-ti- ónis, Dó-num fac remissi- ó-

nis, Ante dí- em ra-ti- ónis. Ingemísco, tamquam

ré-us : Cúlpa rúbet vúltus mé- us : Suppli-cánti párce

Dé- us. Qui Ma-rí- am absolvísti, Et latró-nem exau-

dísti, Mí-hi quoque spem dedísti. Préces mé-ae non sunt

dignae : Sed tu bó-nus fac benígne, Ne per-énni crémer

ígne. Inter óves ló- cum praésta, Et ab haédis me

sequéstra, Stá-tu-ens in párte déxtra. Confu-tá-tis ma-

ledíctis, Flámmis ácribus addíctis, Vóca me cum be-

nedíctis.   Oro súpplex et acclí-nis,   Cor contrí-tum qua-

si cí-nis :   Gé-re cúram mé- i fí-nis.   Lacrimósa dí- es

ílla,   Qua resúrget ex   favílla   Judi-cándus hó- mo

ré- us : Hú- ic ergo pár- ce Dé-us.   Pí- e Jésu Dómine,

dóna é- is réqui- em.   A- men.

Dies irae, dies illa,	Day of wrath, that day
Solvet saeclum in favilla:	Will dissolve the earth in ashes
Teste David cum Sibylla.	As David and the Sibyl bear witness.
Quantus tremor est futurus,	What dread there will be
Quando judex est venturus,	When the Judge shall come
Cuncta stricte discussurus!	To strictly judge all things.
Tuba mirum spargens sonum	A trumpet, spreading a wondrous sound
Per sepulcra regionum,	Through the graves of all lands,
Coget omnes ante thronum.	Will drive mankind before the throne.
Mors stupebit et natura,	Death and Nature shall be astonished
Cum resurget creatura,	When all creation rises again
Judicanti responsura.	To answer to the Judge.
Liber scriptus proferetur,	A book, written in, will be brought forth
In quo totum continetur,	In which is contained everything that is,
Unde mundus judicetur.	Out of which the world shall be judged.
Judex ergo cum sedebit,	When therefore the Judge takes His seat
Quidquid latet apparebit:	Whatever is hidden will reveal itself.
Nil inultum remanebit.	Nothing will remain unavenged.

Quid sum miser tunc dicturus?	What then shall I say, wretch that I am,
Quem patronum regaturus?	What advocate entreat to speak for me,
Cum vix justus sit securus?	When even the righteous may hardly be secure?
Rex tremendae majestatis,	King of awful majesty,
Qui salvandos salvas gratis,	Who freely savest the redeemed,
Salva me, fons pietatis.	Save me, O fount of goodness.
Recordare Jesu pie,	Remember, blessed Jesus,
Quod sum causa tuae viae	That I am the cause of Thy pilgrimage,
Ne me perdas illa die.	Do not forsake me on that day.
Quaerens me, sedisti lassus:	Seeking me Thou didst sit down weary
Redemisti crucem passus:	Thou didst redeem me, suffering death of the cross,
Tantus labor non sit cassus.	Let not such toil be in vain.
Juste judex ultionis,	Just and avenging Judge,
Donum fac remissionis,	Grant remission
Ante diem rationis.	Before the day of reckoning.
Ingemisco, tamquam reus:	I groan like a guilty man.
Culpa rubet vultus meus:	Guilt reddens my face.
Supplicanti parce Deus.	Spare a suppliant, O God.
Qui Mariam absolvisti,	Thou who didst absolve Mary Magdalene
Et latronem exaudisti,	And didst hearken to the thief,
Mihi quoque spem dedisti.	To me also hast Thou given hope.
Preces meae non sunt dignae:	My prayers are not worthy,
Sed tu bonus fac benigne,	But Thou in Thy merciful goodness grant
Ne perenni cremer igne.	That I burn not in everlasting fire.
Inter oves locum praesta,	Place me among Thy sheep
Et ab haedis me sequestra,	And separate me from the goats,
Statuens in parte dextra.	Setting me on Thy right hand.
Confutatis maledictis,	When the accursed have been confounded
Flammis acribus addictis,	And given over to the bitter flames,
Voca me cum benedictis.	Call me with the blessed.
Oro supplex et acclinis,	I pray in supplication on my knees.
Cor contritum quasi cinis:	My heart contrite as the dust,
Gere curam mei finis.	Safeguard my fate.
Lacrimosa dies illa,	Mournful that day
Qua resurget ex favilla	When from the dust shall rise
Judicandus homo reus:	Guilty man to be judged.
Huic ergo parce Deus.	Therefore spare him, O God.
Pie Jesu Domine,	Merciful Jesus, Lord
Dona eis requiem.	Grant them rest.
Amen.	Amen.

13

Hildegard of Bingen
O rubor sanguinis (c1150)

Hildegard experienced visions throughout her life. During her youth they were a source of concern and embarrassment; she recalled keeping silent about them as much as possible. However, during her early forties she had a vision in which God instructed her to write down what she saw in her mind. Believing herself not worthy of such honor, she refrained from obeying, but became sick. Finally relenting, she began transcribing her visions and for the next ten years recorded these revelations in a book called the *Scivias*. This divine commission was remarkable, even for an age that respected mysticism. Hildegard's supportive abbot notified ecclesiastical authorities, and the pope sent a delegation to verify her experiences. They brought back a portion of the *Scivias*, which the pope read aloud to assembled church leaders, and Hildegard soon received a papal letter commanding her to write whatever the Holy Spirit revealed. In a letter written late in life, she said her texts were taken directly from the vision, but remarkably she said nothing about the music, which she apparently added at a later time.

O rubor sanguinis is an antiphon dedicated to the memory of St. Ursula, a British princess from the fourth or fifth century. According to tradition, she went on a pilgrimage to Rome accompanied by 11,000 other virgins. Returning home, they were massacred by pagan Huns outside Cologne. Centuries later, the walls encircling that city were expanded, and excavations for the foundations uncovered an ancient Christian burial ground. The authorities were astounded by the sheer number of bones, and interest was renewed in the legendary slaughter. Many of the remains became honored relics at various monasteries, including Disibodenberg, where the youthful Hildegard resided. The text of Hildegard's antiphon calls forth the image of the martyrs' sacred blood and the purity of those virgins, whose flowers were never plucked, whose youthful lives were untouched by evil.

Hildegard of Bingen
O rubor sanguinis (c1150)
CD 1/13

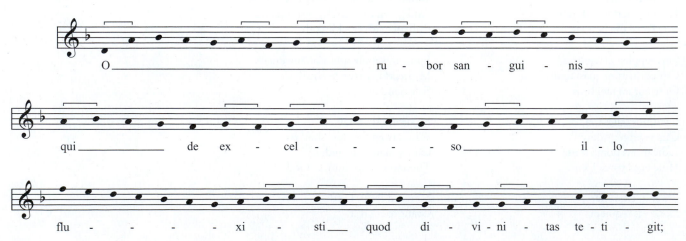

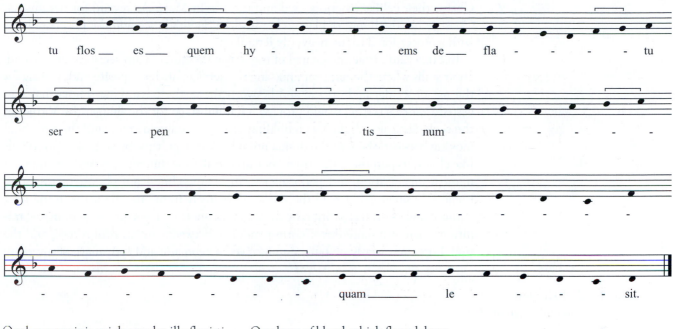

tu flos es quem hy - - - ems de fla - - - tu

ser - - pen - - - - - tis num - - - - - -

- - - - - - - quam le - - - sit.

O rubor sanguinis qui de excelso illo fluxisti	O redness of blood, which flowed down
quod divinitas tetigit;	from on high touched by divinity;
tu flos es quem hyems de flatu serpentis	You are the flower that the wintry breath of
numquam lesit.	the serpent never wounded.

14

Hildegard of Bingen
Excerpts from *Ordo virtutum* (c1150)

There is a rich allegorical tradition in Western civilization that seeks to illustrate the Christian religion's understanding of the battle between good and evil, and the individual's journey from spiritual death to life. Serving a didactic purpose, these works encourage, instruct, and warn the faithful. Three of the most famous of these allegories are Dante's *The Divine Comedy*, John Bunyan's *The Pilgrim's Progress*, and *The Chronicles of Narnia* by C. S. Lewis. Hildegard's *Ordo virtutum* is an early example. As the temporal and spiritual guardian of her abbey, she must certainly have composed this work with the expectation that it would encourage her nuns to remain faithful to their vows, so she addressed the two temptations that are often the most enticing: sensual pleasure and sexual fulfillment. The excerpt provided below is near the beginning of the play.

After a short introduction, the play depicts a Soul that becomes discouraged by the rigors of the straight and narrow path. When she looks back at worldly pleasures, the Devil enters, embraces her, and lures her to his domain. Recalling the Soul's good beginning, the Virtues lament her loss and determine to make a rescue. Thereafter follows a lengthy passage where the fifteen Virtues are introduced one by one. This takes almost half the play, during which interval sins ensnare the Soul with bitter regret. Before the Virtues can whisk the now contrite Soul away, Satan informs them accusingly that virginity is against God's command. Chastity, one of the Virtues, rebukes the Devil by stating that since it was a virgin who brought forth

Christ, their celibacy honors God and the Virgin Mary. As reward for her answer, Chastity has the honor of placing her heel on Satan's head, and the play concludes with a processional to the heavenly Jerusalem.

In Hildegard's time the chapel of the abbey had three main sections: at one end, choir stalls where the nuns sat and sang the service; at the opposite end, seating for the use of secular authorities; and between them, the nave. One scholar has suggested that this setting would provide a natural stage for the drama: the Virtues at the ecclesiastical end, the Devil holding court in the world's end, and the poor Soul moving between them as the drama unfolds. Although this music looks and sounds like chant, its purpose is theatrical, not liturgical. One difference is in the manner of musical organization and performance. In chant, choral antiphons, or responds, frame solo singing, but here the music flows freely from one character to the next without any musical repetition by the choir. In another departure from liturgical tradition, there is a more direct correspondence between the musical setting and the text: Important words are often emphasized by neumatic and melismatic settings.

Hildegard of Bingen
Excerpts from *Ordo virtutum* (c1150)
CD 1/14

Stepitus Diaboli ad Animam illam: Fatue, fatue! Quid prodest tibi laborare? Respice mundum,
et amplectetur te magno honore.

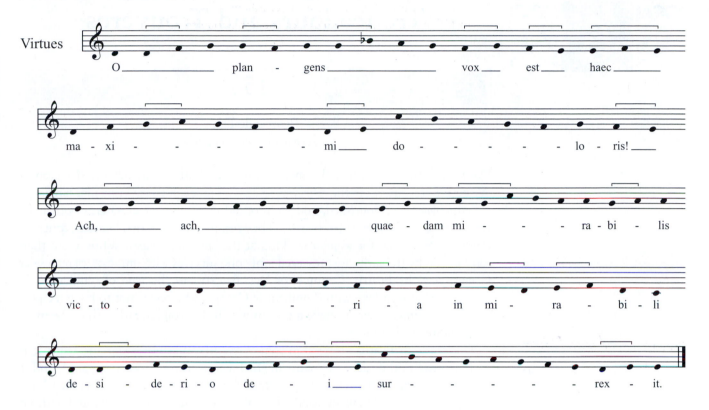

Scientia Dei

Tu nescis, nec vides,
nec sapis illum qui te constituit.

Anima

Deus creavit mundum;
non facio illi iniuriam,
sed volo uti illo!

Strepitus Diaboli ad Animam illam

Fatue, fatue! Quid prodest tibi laborare?
Respice mundum, et amplectetur
te magno honore.

Virtutes

O plangens vox est hec maximi doloris!
Ach, ach, quaedam mirabilis victoria
in mirabili desiderio dei surrexit.

Knowledge of God

You neither know, nor see,
nor taste He who has set you here.

The Soul

God created the world;
I am not doing it ill,
I only want to enjoy it!

Noisy Devil shouting at the Soul

Stupid, stupid! What does hard work get you?
Look to the world, and
great honor will be bestowed upon you.

Virtues

Is this not the most lamentable voice of
greatest sorrow? Ah, ah, a certain wondrous
victory already arose in her wondrous desire
for God.

Chapter 6

Troubadours and Trouvères

15

Beatriz de Dia
A chantar m'er (c1175)

During the twelfth century the most cultured and artistically advanced region of Western Europe north of the Alps was southern France. Here a vernacular language, called *langue d'oc,* flourished, and so, too, did creative poet-musicians both male (troubadours), and female (trobairitz). They composed love songs, laments, songs for crusaders and songs for women working at the spinning wheel. While more than forty poems by trobairitz are preserved, only one survives with music, *A chantar m'er* (*I must sing*) by Beatriz, Countess of Dia. Beatriz was the wife of Guillaume de Poitiers, but was in love with Raimbaut of Orange, who seems not to have reciprocated her feelings. Here we have a case in which the woman, rather than the man, feels slighted by her lover.

The music of Beatriz's song is in some ways like that of Gregorian chant. It is monophonic (although instruments might have been used to accompany), and it seems to have no clear-cut meter or rhythm (though the stresses of the text may have provided some metric organization). It is also predominantly stepwise and without large leaps or chromatic inflections. On the other hand, like much of this vernacular music, it is organized in clearly repeating patterns, something rarely found in plainsong. The seven lines of the poem produce the musical pattern **ABABCDB**. Finally, virtually all of the songs of the troubadours and trouvères make use of strophic form. This song has five stanzas, although only the first is given here and on the recording.

 Beatriz de Dia
A chantar m'er (c1175)
CD 1/15

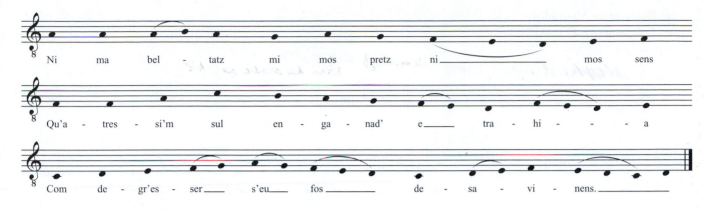

Ni   ma   bel - tatz   mi   mos   pretz   ni_____   mos   sens

Qu'a - tres - si'm   sul   en - ga - nad'   e_____   tra - hi - _ - _ - a

Com   de - gr'es - ser____   s'eu____   fos_____   de - sa - vi - nens._____

A chantar m'er de so qu'eu no volria

Tant me rancur de lui cui sui amia

Car eu l'am mais que nulha ren que sia

Vas lui no'm val merces ni cortezia

Ni ma beltatz ni mos pretz ni mos sens

Qu'atressi'm sui enganad' e trahia

Com degr'esser s'eu fos desavinens.

I must sing of that which I'd rather not,

So bitter do I feel toward him

Whom I love more than anything.

But with him kindness and courtliness get
  me nowhere,

Neither my beauty, nor my worth, nor my
  intelligence.

In this way am I cheated and betrayed,

Just as I would be if I were ugly.

16

Bernart de Ventadorn
Can vei la lauzeta (c1165)

This song is one of the oldest troubadour melodies. Three different manuscripts include Bernart's text and tune *Can vei la lauzeta*, and the melody is used for several other poems as well. One result of this popularity is that there are a number of variants between the different manuscripts. It is impossible to tell which version was originally composed by Bernart or if he wrote them all at different times. More than likely, some of the variants were based on the memory of the scribe rather than the precise intention of the composer.

One of the questions a performer must address is which version to sing. The transcription provided in the anthology comes from a late thirteenth-century manuscript that was made in the south of France.[1] In this version the song only repeats one musical phrase (**D**), giving it the following musical form: **ABCDEFDG**. However, the soloist featured on the recording draws freely from four different sources, mixing and matching phrases from the different manuscripts to suit his own performance instincts. Another performance decision regards the use of accompaniment. Scholars debate whether or not these songs were sung with instruments, but the one absolute certainty is that troubadours did not notate any accompaniment. Since it cannot be proven whether instruments were or were not used, modern performers are left to make their own decisions.

---

[1] A page from this manuscript is reproduced in the *New Grove II* (vol. 25, p. 809). *Can vei la lauzeta* is not on the page, but other songs by Ventadorn are, and his name (B. Ventadorn) is at the top of the manuscript page.

Bernart de Ventadorn
Can vei la lauzeta (c1165)
CD 1/16

[handwritten:] strophic design — same piece of music over and over. It's his music only his

[handwritten left margin:] Many variant versions / realisations see also Narcus "Early Med Music"

Can vei la lauze-ta mo-ver De joi sas a-las con-tral rai,

Que s'o-bli-da lais-sa cha-zer Per la dos-sor c'al cor li vay,

Ai las cal en-ve-ia m'en ve De qui q'eu ve-ya jau-zi-on,

Me-ra-vil-las ai, car des-se Lo cor de de-si-rer no'm fon.

I

Can vei la lauzeta mover
de joi sas alas contral rai,
que s'oblid' e's laissa chazer
per la doussor c'al cor li vai,
ai! tan grans enveya m'en ve
de cui qu'eu veya jauzion,
meravilhas ai, car desse
lo cor de dezirer no'm fon.

When I see the lark beating
its wings joyfully against the sun's rays,
which then swoons and swoops down
because of the joy in its heart,
oh! I feel such jealousy
for all those who have the joy of love,
that I am astonished
that my heart does not immediately melt
with desire!

II

Ai, las! tan cuidava saber
d'amor, e tan petit en sai,
car eu d'amar no'm posc tener
celeis don ja pro non aurai.
Tout m'a mo cor, e tout m'a me,
e se mezeis e tot lo mon;
e can' se'm tolc, no'm laisset re
mas dezirer e cor volon.

Alas! I thought I knew so much
of love, and I know so little;
for I cannot help loving a lady
from whom I shall never obtain any favor.
She has taken away my heart and myself,
and herself and the whole world;
and when she left me, I had nothing left
but desire and a yearning heart.

III

Anc non agui de me poder
ni no fui meus de l'or' en sai
que'm laisset en sos olhs vezer

en un miralh que mout me plai.
Mirahls, pus me mirei en te,
m'an mort li sospir de preon,
c'aissi'm perdei com perdet se
lo bels Narcisus en la fon.

I have no power over myself,
and have not had possession of myself
since the time when she allowed me to look
    into her eyes
in a mirror which I like very much.
Mirror, since I was reflected in you,
deep sighs have killed me,
for I caused my own ruin, just as
fair Narcissus caused his by looking in the
    fountain.

IV

De las domnas me dezesper;
ja mais en lor no'm fiarai;
c'aissi com las solh chaptener,
enaissi las deschaptenrai.
Pois vei c'una pro no m'en te
vas leis que'm destrui e'm cofon,
totas las dopt'e las mescre,
car be sai c'atretals se son.

I despair of ladies;
I shall not trust them ever again;
just as I used to defend them,
now I shall condemn them.
Since I see that one of them does not help me
against her[2] who is ruining and destroying me
I fear them all and have no faith in them,
for I know they are all the same.

V

D'aisso's fa be femna parer
ma domna, pare qu'e'lh o retrai,
car no vol so c'om deu voler,
e so c'om li deveda, fai.
Chazutz sui en mala merce,
et ai be faih co'l fols en pon;
e no sai per que m'esdeve,
mas car trop puyei contra mon.

My lady shows herself to be [merely] a woman
(and that is why I reproach her)
in that she does not want what one should
   want,
and does what is forbidden her.
I have fallen out of favor,
and have acted like the fool on the bridge;
and I do not know why this has happened
   to me,
unless it was because I tried to climb too high.

VI

Merces es perduda, per ver,
et eu non o saubi anc mai,
car cilh qui plus en degr'aver

no'n a ges, et on la querrai?
A! can mal sembla, qui la ve,

qued aquest chaitiu deziron

que ja ses leis non aura be,
laisse morir, que no l'aon!

Mercy is gone, that is sure,
and I never received any of it,
for she who should have the most mercy has
   none,
and where else should I seek it?
Oh! how difficult it is for a person who sees
   her
to imagine that she would allow to die this
   poor yearning wretch,
and would not help the man
who can have no help but her!

VII

Pus ab midons no'm pot valer
precs ni merces ni'l dreihz qu'eu ai,
ni a leis no ven a plazer
qu'eu l'am, ja mais no'lho o dirai.

Aissi'm part de leis e'm recre;
mort m'a, e per mort li respon,
e vau m'en, pus ilh no'm rete,

chaitius, en issilh, no sai on.

Tristans, ges no'n auretz de me,
qu'eu m'en vau, chaitius, no sai on.

De chantar me gic e'm recre,
e de joi e d'amor m'escon.

Since pleas and mercy and my rights
cannot help me to win my lady,
and since it does not please her
that I love her, I shall speak to her about it
   no more.
So I am leaving her and her service;
she has killed me, and I reply with death,
and I am going sadly away, since she will
   not accept
my service, into exile, I do not know where.

Tristan, you will hear no more of me,
for I am going sadly away, I do not know
   where.
I am going to stop singing,
and I flee from love and joy.

[2] Perhaps a reference to the goddess of Love.

Trans. from Hendrik van der Werf, *The Chansons of the Troubadours and Trouvères*, (Utrecht: A Oosthoek, 1972), 91–95.

17

Richard the Lionheart
Ja nuns hons pris ne dira (1192–1194)

King Richard I of England was the ruler of the largest, most powerful realm in twelfth-century Europe. He was a lifelong lover of music; composing music and writing poetry had been a part of his early education. As king, he took an active interest in the singing of the royal chapel, even walking around during service and motivating his choir by vocal encouragement and hand gestures to sing their utmost. Once, when on crusade in the Holy Land, he asked the brother of the Moslem general Saladin to send a musician to sing examples of Arabic music. Richard's chroniclers state that he found it most enjoyable—a clear demonstration of his eclectic tastes. At another point during this Third Crusade, the French troops sang a rude song about Richard, and he reportedly made up an equally insulting song about them on the spot.

While returning home from Jerusalem, Richard, the king of England and ruler of half the lands of France, was kidnapped by the Austrians and held for ransom. The king of France was overjoyed, and Richard's brother John, acting regent of England, was more than delighted, to extend Richard's absence as long as possible. So Richard languished in jail, and it is believed that he relieved some of the tedium by composing *Ja nuns hons pris ne dira*. The musical setting is not nearly as complex as the songs by Beatriz de Dia and Bernart de Ventadorn. The phrase structure can be represented by the letters **AAB**. Both phrases alternate their cadences between G and A. Although here we have a clear example of a song in the Aeolian mode (with a final of A), not until almost four hundred years later would that mode be formally recognized by music theorists.

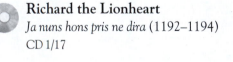

Richard the Lionheart
Ja nuns hons pris ne dira (1192–1194)
CD 1/17

Ja nuns hons pris ne dira sa raison
Adroitement, se dolantement non.
Mais par esfort puet il faire chançon,
Mout ai amis, mais povre sunt li don.
Honte i avront, se por ma reançon,

Sui ça deus yvers pris.

Ce sevent bien mi home et mi baron,
Ynglois, Normanz, Poitevin et Gascon
Que je n'ai nul si povre compaignon
Que je lessaisse, por avoir, en prison.
Je nou di mie por nule retraçon,
Car encor sui pris.

Or sai je bien de voir, certeinnement
Que je ne pris ne ami ne parent,
Quant on me faut por or ne por argent.
Mout m'est de moi, mès plus m'est de ma gent;
Qu'après ma mort avront reprochement,
Se longuement sur pris.

N'est pas mervoille se j'ai le cuer dolant,
Quant mes sires mest ma terre en torment.
S'il li membrast de nostre soirement
Que nos feïsmes andui communement,
Je sai de voir que ja trop longuement
Ne seroie ça pris.

Ce sevent bien Angevin et Torain,
Cil bacheler qui or sont riche et sain,
Qu'encombrez sui loing d'aus, en autre main.
Forment m'aidessent, mais il n'en oient grain.
De beles armes sont ore vuit et plain,
Por ce que je sui pris.

Mes compaignons que j'amoie et que j'ain,
Cés de Chaën et cés de Percherain:
Di lor, chançon, qu'il ne sunt pas certain.
C'onques vers aus ne oi faus cuer ne vain.
S'il me guerroient, il feront que vilain,
Tant con je serai pris.

Truly, a captive doesn't speak his mind
fully, unless he voices a heavy heart.
But with effort he can make a song.
I have many friends, but poor are their gifts.
What a disgrace it will be, if for lack of
     ransom,
I am held here for two winters.

English and Normans, men of Aquitaine,
Well know they all who homage owe to me
That not my lowliest comrade in campaign
Should pine thus, had I gold to set him free;
To none of them would I reproachful be
Yet—I am prisoner here!

This have I learned, here thus unransomed left,
That he whom death or prison hides from sight,
Of kinsmen and of friends is clean bereft;
Woe's me! but greater woe on these will light,
Yea, sad and full of shame will be their plight
If long I languish here.

No marvel is it that my heart is sore
While my lord tramples down my land, I trow;
Were he but mindful of the oath we swore
Each to the other, surely do I know
That thus in duress I should long ago
Have ceased to languish here.

And they, my knights of Anjou and Touraine
Well know they, who now sit at home at ease,
That I, their lord, in far-off Allemaine
Am captive. They should help to my release;
But now their swords are sheathed and rust in peace,
While I am prisoner here.

My comrades whom I loved and still do love
The lords of Perche and of Caïeux
Strange tales have reached me that are hard to prove;
I ne'er was false to them; for evermore
Vile would men count them, if their arms they bore
'Gainst me, a prisoner here!

Trans. of stanzas 2–6 by John Gillingham, *Richard I* (New Haven: Yale University Press, 1999), 242–243.

Chapter

Early Polyphony

18

Anonymous
Viderunt Hemanuel (c1125)

Two ways medieval musicians could creatively express their devotion during the liturgy of the Office and Mass were through verbal and musical additions to existing chant. As we have seen (Chapter 5), tropes, sequences, and the liturgical drama were primarily textual elaborations to the chant, although there was a musical component, because they were sung. Still, these elaborations did not alter the monophonic character of chant. Polyphonic music, however, was created when singers simultaneously imposed another line of music upon the existing chant. Such an elaboration, which enriched the existing chant's sonic character, was known as organum. Organum was usually sung by soloists, not the full choir.

Viderunt Hemanuel combines trope and organum into one setting. Both organum and trope occur during the cantor's intonation of the Gradual *Viderunt omnes* (see no. 8). The organum begins with the opening word and concludes at the end of the trope's text, but the trope is inserted between the first and second words of the chant: "Viderunt [trope text] omnes fines terrae." As expected in organum at this time, the chant is present in the lower part. However, after the three notes required for "Viderunt" are sung, the lower part has new music until the end of the trope ("natum in palacio"). The entire upper part is a new musical line. Because the soloists stop singing at the conclusion of the trope, the organum also ceases when the choir enters with the remainder of the Gradual.

 **Anonymous**
Viderunt Hemanuel (c1125)
CD 1/18

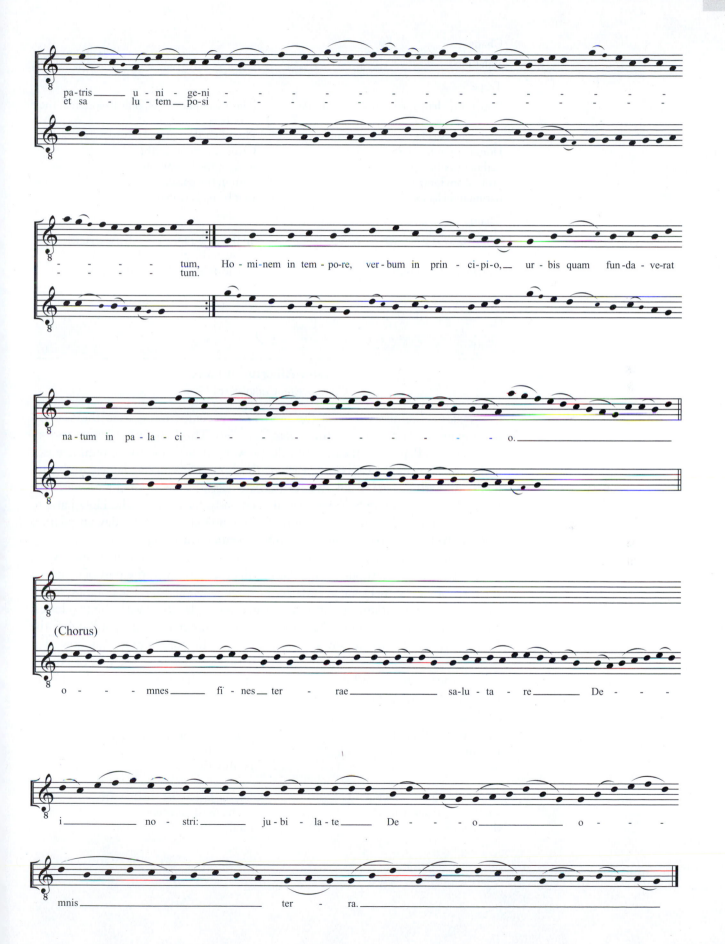

Chant

Viderunt

Trope

[Viderunt] Hemanuel patris unigenitum;	[Have seen] Emanuel, only begotten of the father;
In ruinam Israel et salutem positum.	Placed for the fall and salvation of Israel.
Hominem in tempore,	Created man on earth,
verbum in principio;	word at the beginning;
urbis quam fundaverat,	born in the palace
natum in palacio.	that he had created.

Chant

omnes fines terrae salutare Dei nostri:	all the ends of the earth have seen the salvation of our God:
jubilate Deo omnis terra.	sing joyfully to God, all the earth.

19

Master Albertus of Paris
Congaudeant Catholici (c1150)

Congaudeant Catholici is one of the most famous compositions from the twelfth-century manuscript known as the *Codex Calixtinus*. This book, named after its supposed author, Pope Calixtus II, is an eclectic work. In addition to containing music and liturgy for religious services, particularly those honoring St. James, it also includes an early legend about Roland (Charlemagne's famous knight), a narrative telling how the body of St. James was miraculously carried from the Holy Land to western Spain, and a medieval version of Michelin's guidebook for devout pilgrims making the journey to the Spanish church of Santiago de Compostela.

The music in this manuscript was not composed in Spain, but in France. *Congaudeant Catholici* is attributed to a Master Albertus, who held the post of cantor at the cathedral of Notre Dame in Paris. In the original manuscript, the notation of this three-voice composition is given not on three staves, but two, with the two lowest parts sharing the same staff. These two voices are differentiated by ink color; the lowest part in the transcription was notated in red. This composition also shows that medieval musicians were more concerned with consonance at the end of phrases than at the beginning. While some phrases open with harmonic seconds and thirds, they all close with perfect unisons, fifths, or octaves.

Congaudeant Catholici,	Let the faithful rejoice together,
laetentur cives coelici,	and the heavenly citizens,
die ista.	on this day.
Clerus pulchris carminibus	Let the priests devote themselves
studeat atque cantibus	to the words and music,
die ista.	on this day.

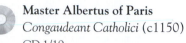

Master Albertus of Paris
Congaudeant Catholici (c1150)
CD 1/19

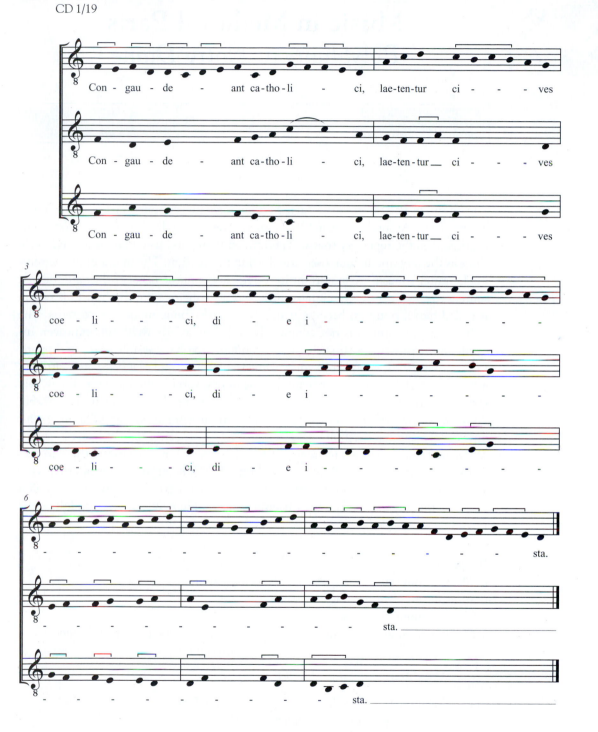

Chapter 8

Music in Medieval Paris
Polyphony at Notre Dame

20

Leoninus
Viderunt omnes (c1170)

Polyphony in Paris during the high Middle Ages was centered at the cathedral of Notre Dame. Around the year 1280, a music theorist, today known as Anonymous IV, described the repertory that was performed there, and listed Leoninus and Perotinus as the prominent composers involved in its creation. The manuscripts preserving Leoninus's music are important in the history of music because they are the first sources to contain a system for measuring and notating musical rhythm. This system is called modal notation because it involves six rhythmic modes, or patterns. The polyphony of Leoninus is not completely and consistently rhythmic, however. Indeed, most of it—the portions in pure organum—involve a sustained tenor supporting a rather free-flowing upper voice. Only the less frequent clausulae are written in a style in which both voices are carefully measured, a style called discant. Today, performers of this repertory generally agree on how to sing the sections in discant, but disagree on the extent to which the sections in pure organum should be sung with any sort of measured rhythm.

Viderunt omnes, as we have seen (MWC, Chapter 8), is a setting of the solo portions of the Gradual of the Mass for Christmas Day. The musical style alternates between *organum purum* and discant (sung by the soloists) and monophonic chant (sung by the full choir). The brief listening guide here may allow you to follow the recording more closely.

Respond

0:00	Organum sung by soloists	*Viderunt*
0:49	Discant clausula sung by soloists	*om-*
0:57	Organum sung by soloists	*nes*
1:23	Chant sung by full choir	*fines terrae salutare Dei nostri; jubilate Deo omnis terra.*

Verse

2:30	Organum sung by soloists	*Notum fecit*
3:00	Discant clausula sung by soloists	*Do-*
3:35	Organum sung by soloists	*minus salutare suum: ante conspectum gentium relevavit*
6:21	Chant sung by full choir	*justitiam suam.*
6:40	(The respond is then repeated.)	

Leoninus
Viderunt omnes (c1170)
CD 1/20

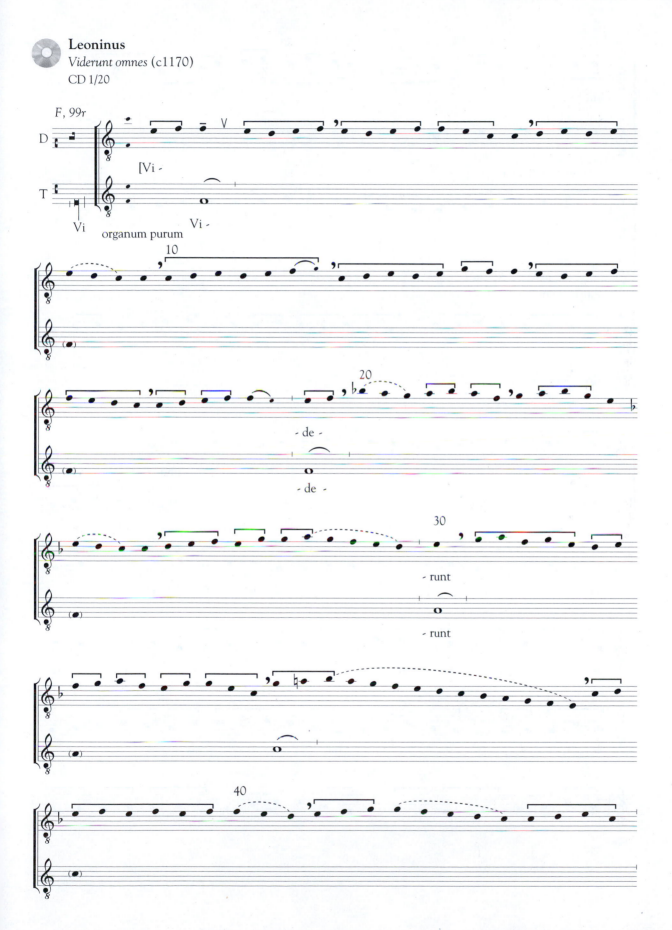

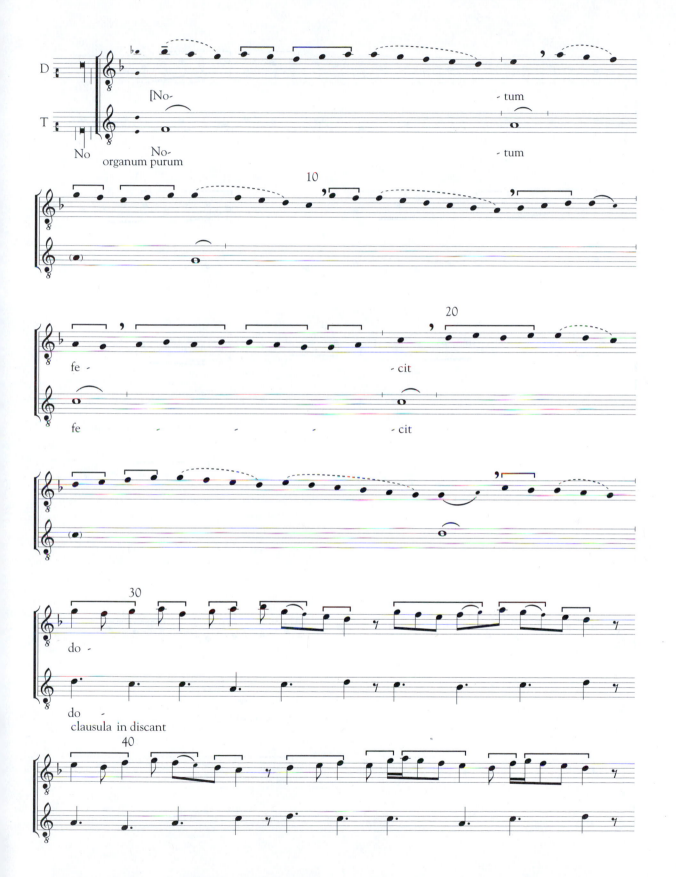

- mi -

- mi -

- nus

organum purum

- nus

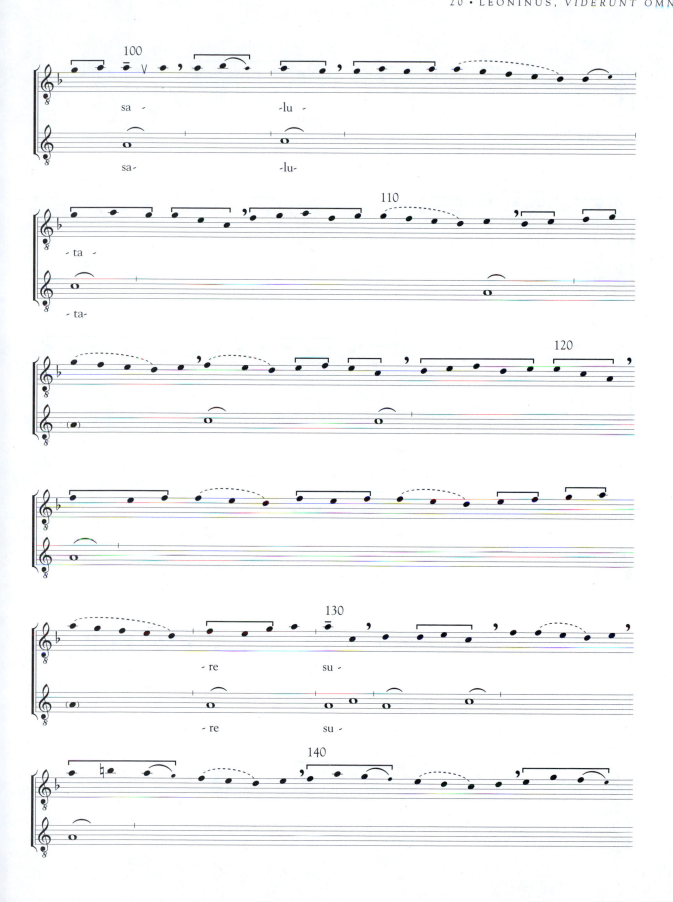

100

sa -   -lu -

sa-   -lu-

110

- ta -

- ta-

120

130

- re   su -

- re   su -

140

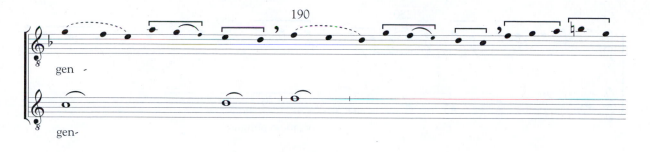

gen -
gen-

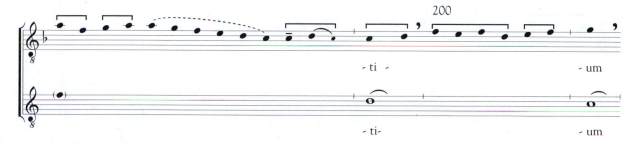

- ti -   - um
- ti-   - um

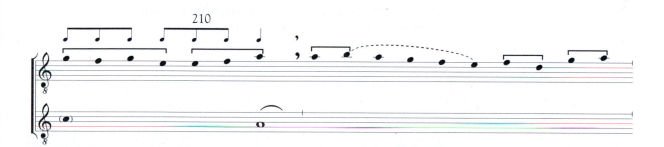

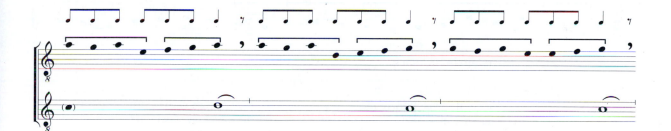

re -   - ve -   - la -
re -   - ve -   - la -
clausula in discant

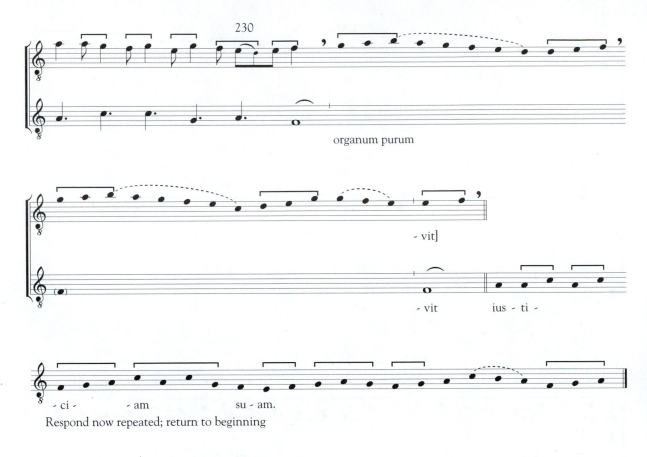

230

organum purum

- vit]

- vit   ius - ti -

- ci -   - am   su - am.

Respond now repeated; return to beginning

Viderunt omnes fines terrae salutare Dei nostri: jubilate Deo omnis terra.	All the ends of the earth have seen the salvation of our God; sing joyfully to God, all the earth.
Notum fecit Dominus salutare suum: ante conspectum gentium revelavit justitiam suam.	The Lord hath made known His salvation; his righteousness he has shown to all the people.

21

Perotinus the Great
Viderunt omnes (1198)

Turning to Perotinus's setting of the same Gradual for Christmas Day, we see a completely different sort of work. Now, instead of just the chant and a single added upper voice, there are three newly created upper voices. These, in addition to the chant in the tenor, are labeled in the modern score Duplum, Triplum, and Quadruplum (D, Tr, and Q). Equally important, all the upper voices are now strictly measured, even in the organum sections. When writing for just two voices, a careful coordination of the rhythm is perhaps not so important. But when writing for four independent voices, rhythmic organization is essential to avoid musical chaos. In addition, not only are the upper voices carefully measured, they are well coordinated. Look closely at the musical phrases at the beginning of the piece and notice the frequent repetition and exchange of the melodic units. Here we can perhaps sense a composer at work, planning and manipulating these cell-like patterns. Perotinus has created a grand and glorious work out of short modular units, all seemingly thought-out carefully in advance. Once again, the brief listening guide below may help you follow the unfolding of this lengthy piece.

Respond

0:00	Organum sung by soloists	*Viderunt*
2:30	Discant clausula sung by soloists	*om-*
2:40	Organum sung by soloists	*nes*
3:48	Chant sung by full choir	*fines terrae salutare Dei nostri: jubilate Deo omnis terra.*

Verse

4:46	Organum sung by soloists	*Notum fecit*
7:05	Discant clausula sung by soloists	*Dominus*
7:40	Organum sung by soloists	*salutare suum: ante conspectum gentium relevavit*
10:10	Chant sung by full choir	*justitiam suam.*

(The respond may then be repeated.)

Perotinus the Great
Viderunt omnes (1198)
CD 1/21

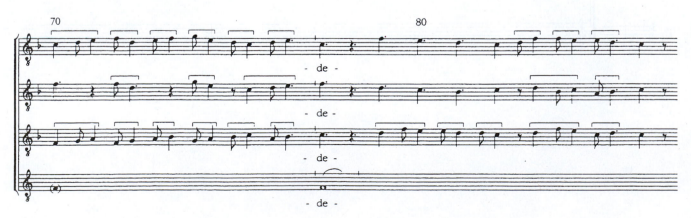

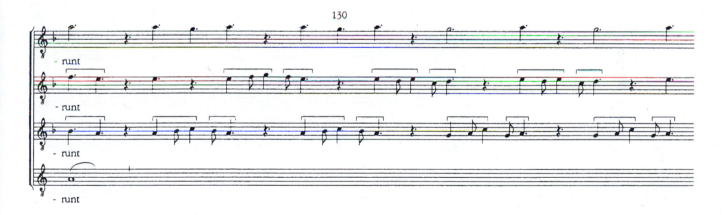

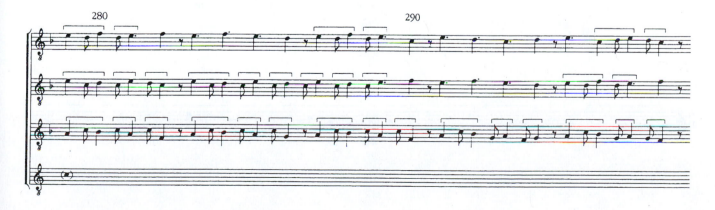

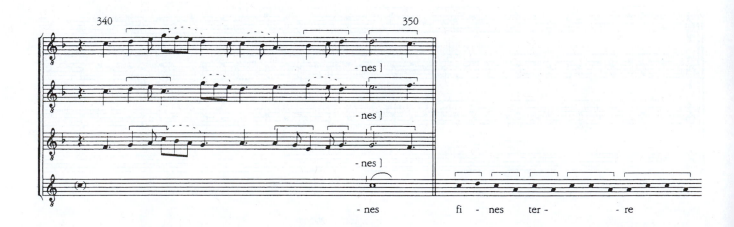

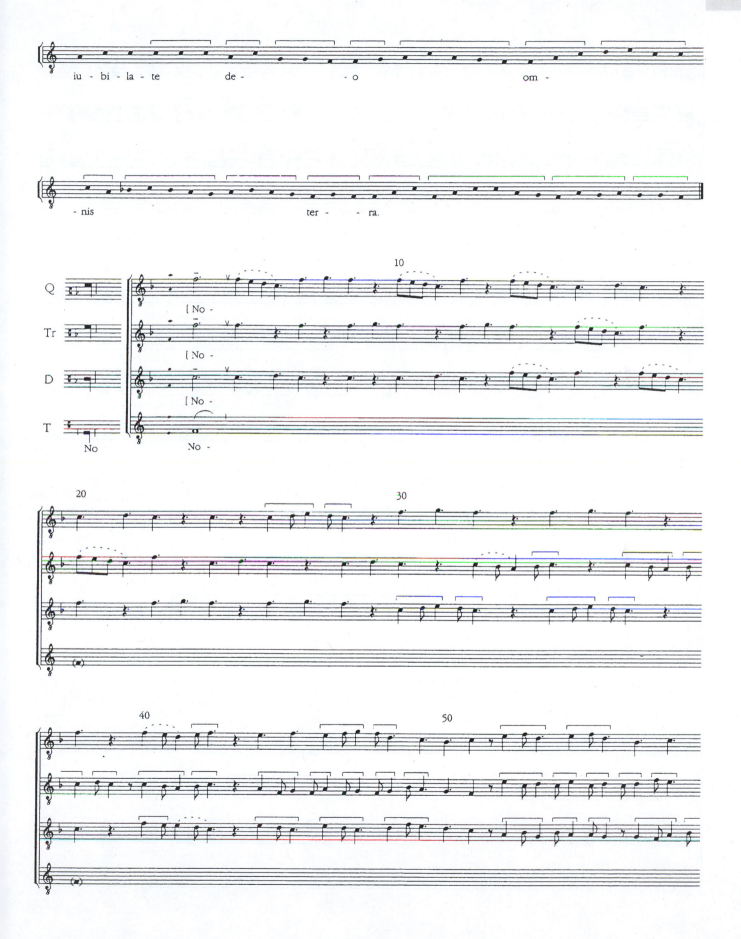

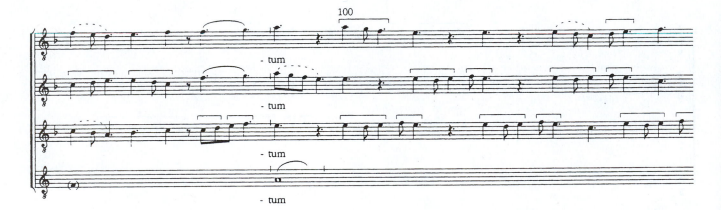

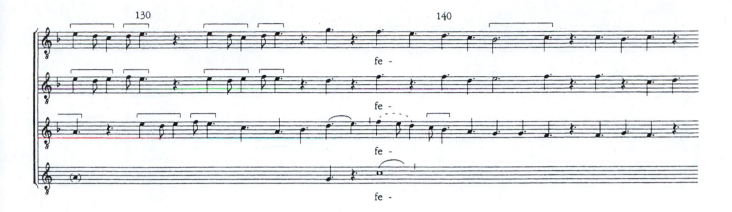

fe -

fe -

fe -

fe -

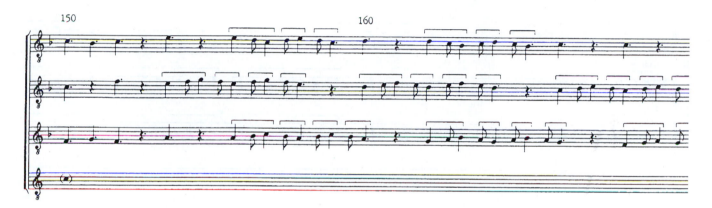

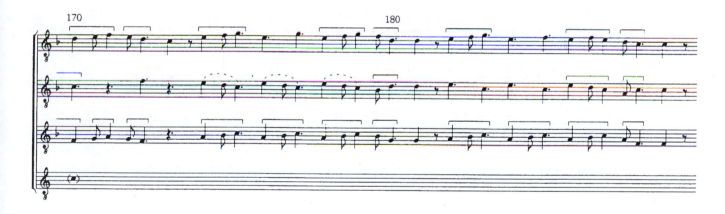

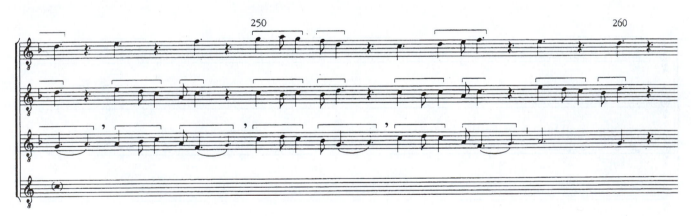

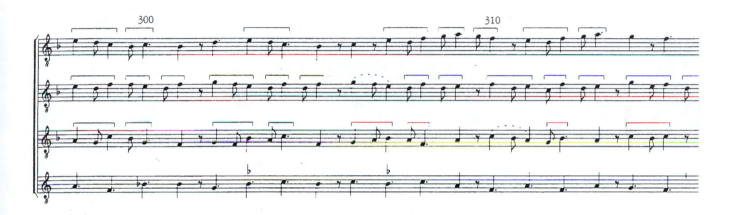

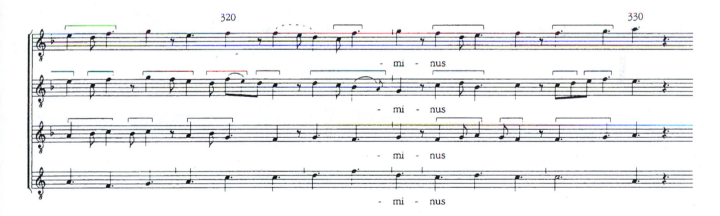

- mi - nus

- mi - nus

- mi - nus

- mi - nus

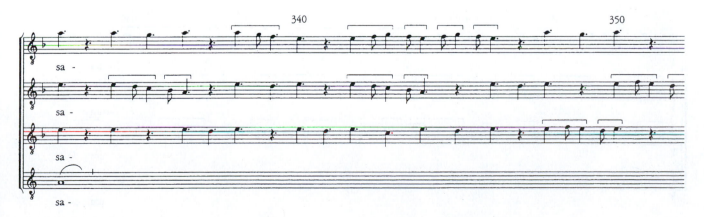

sa -

sa -

sa -

sa -

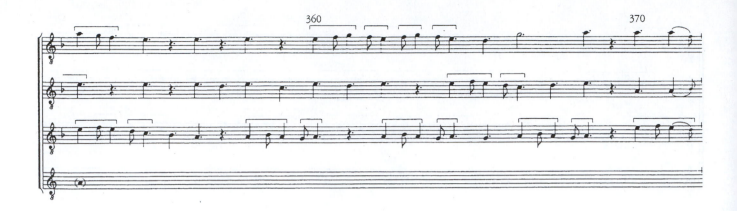

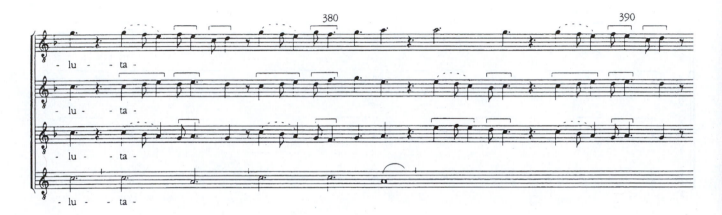

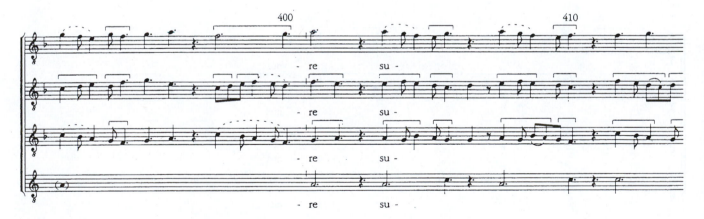

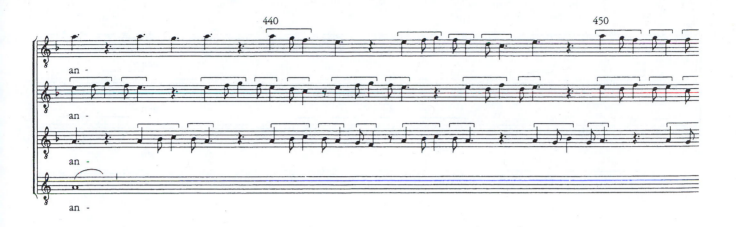

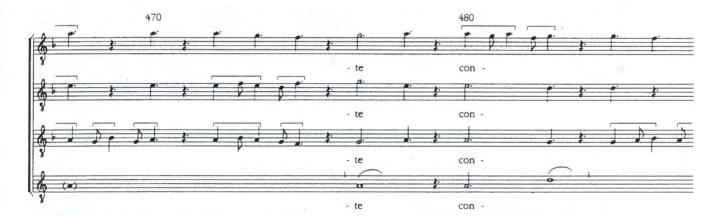

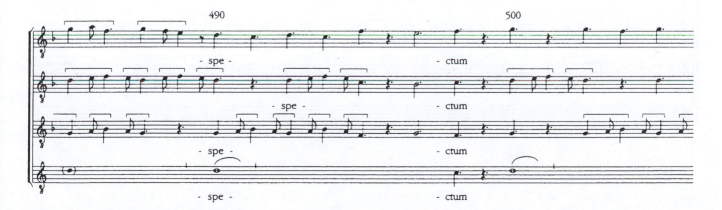

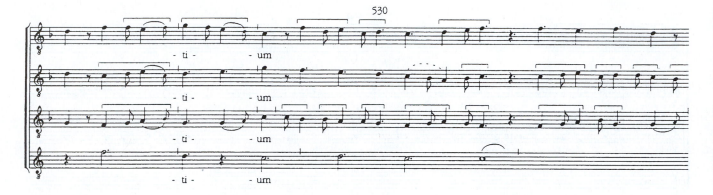

580

- vit]

- vit]

- vit]

- vit.   iu - sti -

- ci - am   su - am.   Vi - de - runt *etc.*

Viderunt omnes fines terrae	All the ends of the earth have seen
salutare Dei nostri:	the salvation of our God;
jubilate Deo omnis terra.	sing joyfully to God, all the earth.
Notum fecit Dominus salutare suum:	The Lord hath made known His salvation;
ante conspectum gentium revelavit	his righteousness he has shown to all the
justitiam suam.	people.

Music in the Cathedral Close and University
Conductus and Motet

22

Anonymous
Orientis partibus (c1200)

The conductus was a genre of extra-liturgical polyphony that emerged during the twelfth century. The term "extra-liturgical" means that the conductus did not belong to the "regular" liturgy of the canonical hours and Mass. Instead, the clergy sang a conductus as it processed into and out of the church, up to the pulpit for an after-noon sermon, or to the refectory for an evening meal, among other places. While some conducti were monophonic, most were polyphonic, being conceived for two, three, or four voices. By the thirteenth century the polyphonic conductus had developed a unique trait: unlike all the other polyphonic genres from the period, it was newly composed in all voices—there was no pre-existing Gregorian chant sounding forth in the tenor. Most conducti were strophic, and the subject matter dealt with Christmas or Easter. Indeed, the lasting legacy of the conductus was that it was an early progenitor of the Christmas carol—strophic compositions treating in one way or another the subject of the Nativity and often incorporating hints of popular tunes.

One conductus that ultimately became a Christmas carol is *Orientis partibus*. Originally *Orientis partibus* was sung as a processional piece as part of the Christmas revels called the Feast of Fools. Because the lowest of the three parts has the smoothest rhythm, the most conjunct voice leading, and outlines the C major triad, this bottom voice sounds the most tuneful and "popular" to our modern ears. Indeed, in the course of the centuries that melody became a well-known English carol, under the title *The Friendly Beast*. Countless musicians have recorded this legacy of the Middle Ages, including the country singer Garth Brooks.

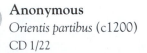

Anonymous
Orientis partibus (c1200)
CD 1/22

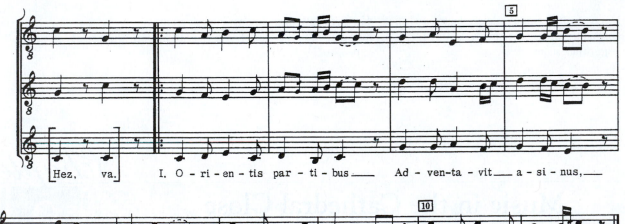

Orientis partibus
Adventavit asinus,
Pulcher et fortissimus,
Sarcinis aptissimus.
Hez, va, hez, sire asne hez!

From Orient lands
Came an ass,
Handsome and most strong,
An excellent beast of burden.
Hey, ho, hey, Sir Ass, hey!

Hic in collibus Sychem	Here in the hills of Sychen,
Iam nutritus sub Ruben,	Already suckled below the Ruben,
Transit per Iördanem,	He crosses through the Jordan
Saliit in Bethleem.	And leaps into Bethlehem.
Hez, va, hez, sire asne hez!	Hey, ho, hey, Sir Ass, hey!
Saltu vincit hynnulos,	With a leap he out-jumped the stag,
Dammas et capreolos,	The antelope and deer,
Super dromedarios	Faster than dromedaries
Velox Madyaneos.	From Media.
Hez, va, hez, sire asne hez!	Hey, ho, hey, Sir Ass, hey!
Aurum de Arabia,	Gold from Arabia,
Thus et myrrham de Saba	Frankincense and Myrrh from Saba,
Tulit in ecclesia	Are borne into the church
Virtus asinaria.	By this excellent Ass.
Hez, va, hez, sire asne hez!	Hey, ho, hey, Sir Ass, hey!
Dum trahit vehicula	While he pulls carts,
Multa cum sarcinula,	Many with small loads,
Illius mandibula	He grinds down the tough fodder
Dura terit pabula.	With the bit.
Hez, va, hez, sire asne hez!	Hey, ho, hey, Sir Ass, hey!
Cum aristis ordeum,	He eats barley, husks and all,
Domedit et carduum,	And thistles.
Triticum a palea	He separates wheat from the chaff
Segregat in area.	On the threshing floor.
Hez, va, hez, sire asne hez!	Hey, ho, hey, Sir Ass, hey!
"Amen," dicas, asine,	"Amen," you say, ass,
Iam satur ex gramine,	Now so full of grass,
"Amen, amen," itera	"Amen, amen," again
Aspernare vetera.	Despising tradition.
Hez, va, hez, sire asne hez!	Hey, ho, hey, Sir Ass, hey!
Eia, frater asine,	Eia, brother Ass,
Unum quod vis elige:	Choose one as you wish:
Carduos vel commede,	Eat wild thistles,
Vel dic: "Iube Domine."	Or read: "Command, O Lord."

Adapted from *Notre-Dame and Related Conductus*, Part 9, *Three-Part Conductus in Related Sources*, ed. by Gordon Anderson (Henryville: Institute of Mediaeval Music, 1986), II–III.

23

Philip the Chancellor
Dic, Christi veritas (c1230)

In contrast to the simple, popular style of the anonymous *Orientis partibus* stands Philip the Chancellor's learned *Dic, Christi veritas*. Take a moment and examine the translation of his text. The numerous allusions seem obscure. But to the clergy at Notre Dame, and the masters and students at the university, all was crystal clear.

Here Philip calls Truth (*Veritas*) to his aid. But where is she hiding: is she in the Valley of Vision (Jerusalem), on the throne of the kings of Egypt, at the court of the wicked Emperor Nero, or in the cave of the misanthropic Timon? Four literary allusions come within four lines, two biblical (from Isaiah and Exodus) and two classical (from Roman history and literature). The parallel—biblical-classical—continues: perhaps Truth is hiding with Moses in the bulrushes (on the Nile) or in the house of Romulus (in Rome), the home of the papal bull, a symbol of the pope's abusive power.[1] The poetic images come fast and furious, but a student in medieval Paris, steeped in the Bible and classical learning, would have understood them all. Philip the Chancellor is preaching to the educated.

Indeed, in *Dic, Christi veritas* music and poetry work in harmony for maximum rhetorical effect. Introducing several of the phrases suggesting where Truth may lie is a *cauda*—a lengthy melisma. The *caudae* serve to introduce separate syntactical units (beginning, in turn, with "Tell us," "Perhaps," and "Or"). The words within each unit come in short, repetitive bursts, as if a spellbinding preacher were at work. The final *cauda* breaks forth on the next-to-last syllable, in the concluding word "fulminante." In this extraordinary musical outburst, one can almost see Philip the Chancellor fulminating against the pope for supporting his antagonists, the faculty of the University of Paris.

Philip the Chancellor
Dic, Christi veritas (c1230)
CD 1/23

---

[1] The term papal "bull" comes from the Latin word *bulla*, the waxen seal, stamped with the papal signet ring, affixed to all his official proclamations.

tas, _____ U - bi nunc ha - bi - tas? _____

(aut) in val - le

vi - si - o - nis, Aut __ in thro - no Pha - ra - o - nis, Aut in _al - to cum Ne - ro - ne,

Aut in _ an - tro cum The-o - ne? Vel _____ (vel) __ in fi -

scel - la _ scir - pe - a Cum Mo - ÿ se plo-ran - te? Vel _____ in do-mo _ Ro -

mu - le - a____ Cum bul - la ful - mi - nan -   - mi -

mu - le - a____   - nan -   - te.____

Dic, Christi veritas,	Tell us, O Truth of Christ,
Dic, cara raritas,	Tell us, O Dear Rarity,
Dic, rara caritas,	Tell us, O Rare Charity,
Ubi nunc habitas?	Where do you dwell now?
Aut in valle visionis,	Perhaps in the Valley of Vision [Palestine],
Aut in throno Pharaonis,	On the throne of the Pharaoh [Egypt]
Aut in alto cum Nerone,	On high with Nero [Rome]
Aut in antro cum Theone?	Or in the cave with Theon [Greece]
Vel in fiscella scirpea	Or in a basket of rushes
Cum Moÿse plorante?	With the plaintive Moses [Hebrew antiquity]
Vel in domo Romulea	Or in the house of Romulus [Rome]
Cum bulla fulminante?	With the thundering bull?

24

Anonymous
a. *Et gaudebit* for Alleluia. *Non vos relinquam* (c1200)
b. *O quam sancta/Et gaudebit* (c1230)
c. *El mois d'avril/O quam sancta/Et gaudebit* (c1230)

The genre of the motet had its beginnings in the early thirteenth century, and it continues to the present day in the works of such composers as John Tavener, Arvo Pärt, and Krzysztof Penderecki, among others. Bach, Mozart, Brahms, and Bruckner all wrote motets as well. Naturally, a genre that has been in use for around eight hundred years has undergone dramatic changes. But its very name, "motet," takes us back to its beginning. The term descends from the French word "*mot*" ("word"), and it suggests the origins of the genre: words were added to preexisting music. Specifically, new text was added to the discant clausula (and substitute clasulae) that was embedded in organum. The text below shows the layout of the organum written for an Alleluia for the Feast of the Ascension: *Alleluia. Non vos reliquam*. The boldface type shows the position of the clausula in discant style, to which words were eventually added to form the motet.

Alleluia————. Non vos relinquam orphanos; vado et venio ad vos **et gaudebit** cor vestrum.
Organum-chant. Organum—————**clausula**—organum—.

(Alleluia: I will not leave you orphans; I come and go among you, and your heart, **it will rejoice**).

The anthology provides three examples that show the evolutionary beginnings of the motet. The first example (24a) is a clausula to be inserted in the organum *Alleluia. Non vos relinquam* at the words "*et gaudebit*" ("it will rejoice"). Notice that the tenor melody (the Gregorian chant) is repeated (beginning at m. 70), and the rhythms to which this chant is set are repeated exactly as well. Although there is no audio for 24a and 24b, they are the lower two voices within the three-voice motet (24c).

Anonymous

a. *Et gaudebit* for Alleluia. *Non vos relinquam* (c1200)

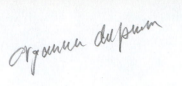

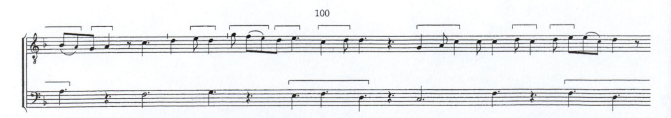

Now we have the same clausula, but with words applied to the upper voice, creating the motet entitled *O quam sancta/Et gaudebit*. Medieval motets are known by the first words of each part, beginning with the uppermost voice. The newly texted second voice (called the motetus, because it has words) sings a Latin poem in praise of the Virgin Mary. Since the tenor is not repeated, this motet is only half as long as the discant clausula given in 24a. Also, the source manuscript comes from Spain, not Paris, and the notes of the tenor differ in some places in both pitch and rhythm from those given in the Parisian sources. These variants are indicated by the asterisks. The essential point, however, is that what was originally an untexted clausula has become a motet rejoicing in the mysteries of the Virgin. The text and translation for this motet are provided in the motetus part for 24c.

b. Anonymous
O quam sancta/Et gaudebit (c1230)

---

[1] Notes in parentheses are variant readings and may be substituted for performance.

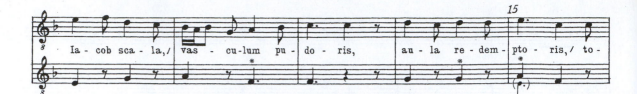

Ia - cob sca - la, / vas - cu - lum pu - do - ris,   au - la re - dem - pto - ris, / to -

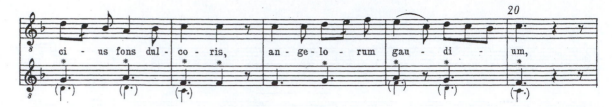

ci - us fons dul - co - ris,   an - ge - lo - rum gau - di - um,

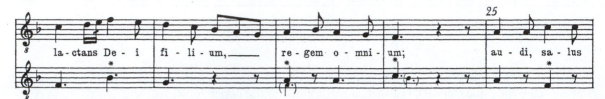

la - ctans De - i   fi - li - um,____   re - gem o - mni - um;   au - di, sa - lus

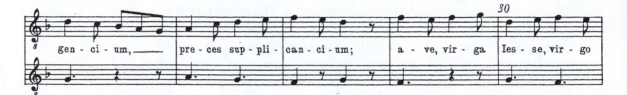

gen - ci - um,____   pre - ces sup - pli - can - ci - um;   a - ve, vir - ga Ies - se, vir - go

no - bi - lis,____   su - per o - mnes ve - ne - ra - bi - lis.

Our last example shows that a third voice (triplum) with a French text describing the beauties of spring was ultimately added to the two-voice motet *O quam sancta/Et gaudebit*. At first glance, this poem seems to have little to do with the spiritual message of the tenor and motetus. Following the method of scriptural exegesis taught in thirteenth-century Paris, however, this new text would be interpreted as an allegory of Christ and the faithful bride (Mary, or perhaps the Christian community).

The charm of *El mois d'avril/O quam sancta/Et gaudebit* rests in the polytextual interplay—verbal counterpoint—between the motetus and triplum. These voices in turn resonate against the spiritual theme of the tenor. The danger, however, is that the piece, while intellectually satisfying, comes off as a jumble of sound. To be effective, each performer must articulate his text clearly so as to convey the meaning of the motet to the audience. But this invites several questions: How was the medieval motet performed? How was the audience able to understand the text? Is this theology or is it music, or both?

Pictorial evidence suggests that the motets of the Middle Ages were sung with just one voice on a part. Indeed, the rapid declamation required by the text would have precluded more than one on a part, with the exception of the tenor. And although the tenor has only a word or two of text, this is no signal that it is to be performed on an instrument: the tenor, too, was undoubtedly sung. How might a performance have gone? It is possible that first the motetus and tenor were sung by themselves, then the triplum and the tenor alone, and finally all three voices together. It is also possible that the separate poems were read purely as poetry prior to the musical performance so as to familiarize the audience with their content. In the case of *El mois d'avril/O quam sancta/Et gaudebit,* allegory and prayer combine to make theology as important as music.

Anonymous
c. *El mois d'avril/O quam sancta/Et gaudebit* (c1230)
CD 1/24

18. Que vos di- roi- e je les nons de tous chans? 19. Il- luec es- toit tous li de- duis d'oi-

Ies- se vir- ga no- bi- lis, 13. su- per o- mnes ve- ne- ra- bi-

- siaus. 20. En- tre qu'es- toie i- lue- ques, si o- ï 21. u- ne pu- ce- le, qui chant en haut cri:

- lis! 14. Spes u- ni- ca, suc- cur- re mi- se- ris!

22. "A- mors no- ve- les font fins a- mans jo- lis!" 23. Tant iert plei- sant 24. et de be- le fai- tu- re,

15. In- e- bri- ans a- ni- mas fons es ad- mi- ra- bi- lis,

25. qu'a i- cel tans 26. n'a- voit on- ques na- tu- re 27. nul pen- sé 28. a si grant biau-

16. que tu- os num- quam mo- ri de- se- ris. 17. O a- ni-

-té. 29. Freche ot la co- lor, 30. blan- che com flor, 31. ieuz vers ri- ans, 32. vis a point co- lo-

-ma, ex [s]or- di- bus vi- lis 18. hanc [13)] Ma- ri- am

fol. 66

-ré, 33. chief blont, lui- sant, 34. me- nu re- cer- ce- lé, 35. bo- che ver- mel- le, dens pe- tis drus se-

vir- gi- nem ex- po- stu- la, 19. ut sit pro te se- du-

fol. 66

-mez, 36. bien or- de- nés, 37. sor- cis vou- tis, bru- nes et bien for- mez: 38. Sa grant biau-

-la 20. ex- o- ra- re fi- li- um 21. pro- pi- ci- um,

8) x2

-té 39. [14)] ne puet bou- che ra- con- ter 40. ne cuer pen- ser. 41. S'a- mor li pri; 42. sos- pi- rant res- pon- di:

22. u- na spes fi- de- li- um. 23. O ge- ni- trix, *gau- de* in

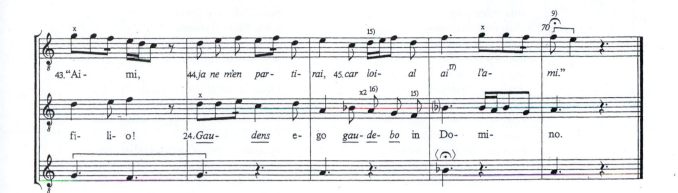

Triplum

El mois d'avril, qu'iver vait departant
que cil oiseil recommencent leur chant
par un matin lés un bois chevauchant
m'en alai, en une sente pensant
m'en entrai, que qu'estoie d'amors en tel
    pensé
lors ne sai, quel part sui torné
et quant en moi regardai et fui aparcevant
en un vergier lors m'en entrai
qui tant estoit deduisant.
Que d'une part chante li rossignol,
d'autre part li mauves,
qu'il n'est mus cuers tant durs ne fust
    resbaudis;
l'espoon et l'aloe chantent si doucement,
la chalandre s'i renvoise ensement:
Que vos diroie je les nons de tous chans?
Illuec estoit tous li deduis d'oisianus.
Entre qu'estoie illueques, si oï
une pucele, qui chant en haut cri:
"Amors moveles font fins amans jolis!"
Tant iert pleasant et de bele faiture
qu'a icel tans n'avoit onques nature
nul pensé a si grant biauté
Freche ot la color blanche com flor
ieus vers rians vis a point coloré
chief blont, luisant, menu recercelé
boche vermelle, dens petis drus semez
bien ordenés sorcis voutis, brunes et bien
    formez:
Sa grant biauté ne peut bouche raconter
ne cuer penser S'amor li pri sospirant
    respondi
"Aimi, ja ne m'en partirai, car loial ai l'ami."

Paraphrase

A young knight rides on a fine spring morning near a forest but loses his way; he finds himself in a delightful garden where birds of every description sing in ways that cannot be described.

There he spies a maiden who sings in a loud voice: "A new love makes true lovers happy!" The maid possesses astonishing beauty: skin as white as a flower, dancing green eyes, ruby lips, blond curly hair, small perfect teeth, well-formed and arching eyebrows. The knight is overcome by her perfection and begs for love, but she rejects him, saying: "I have a loyal sweetheart from whom I will never part."

Motetus

O quam sancta, quam benigna
fulget mater savatoris
laude plena virgo
digna archa Noe,
Jacob scala
vasculum pudoris

Translation

O with what sanctity and kindness
shines the mother of the savior;
a worthy maiden full of praise,
arc of Noah,
ladder of Jacob,
vessel of chastity,

aula redemptoris	palace of the redeemer,
totus fons dulcoris	font of all sweetness,
angelorum **gaudium**.	**joy** of the angels
Lactans Dei filium,	who nursed the Son of God,
regem omnium.	king of all.
Audi, salus gentium	Hear, savior of the people,
preces supplicantium	our prayers of supplication.
Ave, virgo Iesse virga nobilis	Hail, Virgin, bough of the noble Jesse,
super omnes venerabilis.	venerable beyond all.
Spes unica, succurre miseris	Singular hope, aid us miserable ones,
Inebrians animas, fons es admirabilis	you are the admirable font which fills souls to
Que tuos numquam mori deseris	overflowing, who never leaves her people to die;
O anima, ex sordibus vilis	O my soul, beseech this Mary
hanc Mariam virginem expostula	for deliverance from this vile filth,
ut sit pro te sedula	that she may intercede for you,
exorare filium propicium	praying the favor of her son,
una spes fidelium	she who is the one hope of the faithful.
O genitix **gaude** in filio	O mother, **rejoice** in the son,
gaudens ego **gaudebo** in Domino.	**rejoicing** I shall **rejoice** in the Lord.

Tenor

Et **gaudebit**.	And **rejoice**.

25

Anonymous Motet
On parole de batre/A Paris/Frese nouvele (c1280)

Unlike the theologically attuned motet *El mois d'avril/O quam sancta/Et gaudebit*, the all-French three-voice motet *On parole de batre/A Paris/Frese nouvele* has a popular flavor. The tenor is a street cry, not a preexisting Gregorian chant; the voices are all in the vernacular, not Latin; and the text speaks of the pleasures of the flesh, not those of the spirit. Note the continual repetition in the tenor, a phenomenon associated with the compositional technique of isorhythm (same rhythm), which will be discussed in association with Philippe de Vitry (Chapter 11). In this recording the tenor (street cry) is sung first, then the duplum is added, and finally the triplum.

Fresh strawberries = prostitute

Anonymous Motet
On parole de batre/A Paris/Frese nouvele (c1280)
CD 1/25

Triplum

On parole de batre et de vanner	They talk of threshing and winnowing,
Et de foïr et de hanner	of digging and cultivating
Mais ces deduis trop me desplaisent.	but these amusements displease me.
Car il n'est si bone vie que d'estre à aise	Because there is no better life than to be at ease,
De bon cler vin et de chapons	with good clear wine and capon
Et d'estre aveuc bons compaignons	and to be with good companions
Liés et joiaus,	happy and joyful
Chantans, truffans et amorous	singing, joking and loving
Et d'avoir, quant c'on a mestier	and to take, when in need,
Pour solacier	comfort in
Beles dames a devis:	fair ladies.
Et tout ce truev'on à Paris.	All this one finds in Paris.

Motetus

A Paris soir et matin	In Paris, morn and night
Truev'on bon pain et bon cler vin,	one can find good bread and good clear wine
Bone char et bon poisson,	good meat and fish
De toutes guises compaignons,	and every sort of companion,
Sens soutie, grant baudour,	subtle wits and great merriment,
Biaus joiaus dames d'ounour,	handsome, joyful women of honor,
Et si truev'on bien entredeus	and best of all, for the man short of cash,
De menre feur pour homes desiteus.	one can find it at the lowest price.

Tenor

Frese nouvele, muere france, muere muere france!	Fresh strawberries, ripe blackberries, ripe, ripe blackberries!

Chapter 11

Music at the Court of the French Kings

26

Gervès de Bus
Roman de Fauvel (c1314)

The *Roman de Fauvel* is a lengthy satirical poem written by Gervès de Bus in 1314. A few years later, Philippe de Vitry and others expanded the poem, and inserted monophonic and polyphonic chants, conducti, and motets to enrich the poetry. The *Roman de Fauvel* offers a scathing criticism of the government of King Philip IV, known as "the Fair." One of his most enduring innovations was the establishment of a national tax. Since France did not have a tradition of national tax collection, bureaucrats negotiated with each area individually, resulting in bribery and animosity. It was no wonder then that many felt the world had been turned upside down, justice overthrown, and that corruption reigned supreme. In this fable the forces of Flattery,

Avarice, Villainy, Variety (Fickleness), Envy, and Loose Morals (FAUVEL) have been embodied in an ass. The people come to curry favor ("torcher Fauvel" in the original) with this foolish creature. Most of the *Roman de Fauvel* is simply a poem, one likely recited to some sort of musical backdrop or drone. A portion of the poem is included here to provide a sense of the overall *roman*, or story.

Gervès de Bus
Roman de Fauvel (c1314)
CD 1/26

De Fauvel que tant voi torcher	I see so many people curry Fauvel
Doucement sans lui escorcher,	Softly without skinning him,
Sui entréz en merencolie,	I've fallen into a melancholy state
Pour ce qu'est beste si polie.	Because he is so well groomed.
Souvent le voient en pointure	Some often see him in paintings
Tex qui ne sevent sa figure	Who do not know if he represents
Moquerie, sens ou folie.	Mockery, good sense, or folly;
Et pour ce, sanz amphibolie,	And for this reason, without equivocating
Cleremnet dirai de tel beste	In plain language I will speak of this beast
Ce qu'il m'en puet cheoir en teste.	As it comes into my head.
Fauvel ne gist mès en l'estable,	Fauvel no longer lives in a stable
Il a meson plus honorable:	He has a more honorable house:
Haute mengoere demande	A high manger he requests,
Rastelier bel et assez viande	A handsome haystack and plenty of food.
Il s'est herbergiéz en la sale,	He lodges himself in the hall
Pour miex demonstrer sa regale;	The better to demonstrate his royal qualities;
Et non pour quant par sa science	And nevertheless in his wisdom
Es chambres a grant reverence,	In chambers with great honor
Et es gardesrobes souvent	And in privy chambers
Fait toust assembler son couvent,	Often soon assemble all his faithful,
Qui si soingneusement le frote	Who rub him so carefully
Qu'en lui ne puet remanoir crote.	That no dung can remain on him.
Fortune, contraire a raison,	Fortune, contrary to reason,
L'a fait seigneur de sa meson;	Has made him lord of her house
En lui essaucer met grant peine,	And taken great pains to raise him
Car ou palais roial le maine;	Because in the Palais Royal she leads him
De lui fere honorer ne cesse.	To have him honored without ceasing.
Entour Fauvel a si grant presse	Around there is so great a crowd
De gens de toutes nacions	Of people of all nations
Et de toutes condicions	And of all social stations
Que c'est une trop grant merveille;	That it's astonishing to see.
N'i a nul qui ne s'apareille	There is no one there who's not primed
De torcher Fauvel doucement.	To curry Fauvel gently.
Trop i a grant assemblement.	The gathering there is great.
Rois, dus et contes verriez	Kings, dukes and counts of all sorts
Pour torcher Fauvel aliez,	Come to curry Fauvel,
Touz seigneurs temporex et princes	Every prince and temporal lord
Y viennent de toutes provinces,	They come from all lands
Et chevaliers grand et petiz,	And knights great and small
Qui au torchier sont bien fetiz.	To the currying are well delighted.
N'i a, sachéz, ne roi ne conte	To be sure, there is neither king nor count
Qui de torcher Fauvel ait honte.	Who is ashamed to curry Fauvel.
Vicontes, prevos et baillis;	Viscounts, provosts, and sheriffs
A bien torcher ne sont faillis;	To curry well, not are lacking;

Bourgois de bours et de cités	Bourgeoisie of the towns and cities
Torchent par grans subtilités,	Curry with such great subtlety,
Et villains de ville champestre	And rustics from the country towns
Sont empres Fauvel pour li pestre.	Gather round Fauvel to ask him for favors.

27

Anonymous
Quare fremuerunt gentes (c1317)

A feeling of outrage informs the two-voice conductus *Quare fremuerunt gentes*—the people of France seethe over the abuse to which they have been subjected by Fauvel and his minions. The people are raging, however, not in the older *Ars antiqua* style but in that of the newer *Ars nova*. *Quare fremuerunt gentes* was originally a conductus written in the equivalent of modal notation; yet here it is supplied with the new note values and note relationships of the *Ars nova*. It is thus written in mensural notation (sign-specific notation). In the transcription given below, the new note value of the fourteenth century—the minim—is transcribed as a sixteenth-note. There are three minims for each semibreve (eighth-note), two semibreves for each breve (quarter-note), and three breve notes for each long (dotted half-note). Thus the mensuration of *Quare fremuerunt gentes* is perfect prolation, imperfect time, and perfect mode (no maximode is present). The importance of all this is not in the specific details, but rather in the larger issue: now, for the first time in the history of music, composers were able to specify a wide range of rhythmic durations with great precision. Here some measures have just one note, which holds a full measure, while others have twelve notes, which give the appearance of moving by very quickly.

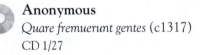

Anonymous
Quare fremuerunt gentes (c1317)
CD 1/27

First couplet

Quare fremuerunt   Why do the peoples
Gentes et populi?   and nations rage?[1]
Quia non viderunt   Because they did not see
Monstra tot oculi   the monsters with their own eyes.

**Music of the first couplet repeated,
but with new ending**

Neque audierunt   Will not the old and young
In orbe seculi   throughout the earth
Senes et parvuli   hear the battles
Prelia que gerunt   that rage

Concluding couplet

Et que sibi querunt   And the kings
Reges et reguli.   and rulers desire?
Hec, inquam, inferunt   All these things, I say,
Fauvel et Falvuli.   Fauvel and his minions have brought
                                        upon us!

[1]The opening sentence plays upon the opening of Psalm 2, "Why do the nations rage against the Lord and His anointed?"

28

Philippe de Vitry
Garrit Gallus/In nova fert/Neuma (c1317)

The complexity of Philippe de Vitry's motet *Garrit Gallus/In nova fert/Neuma* suggests that we are in the midst of the "in crowd" of the university and court, who are creating the most avant-garde art of the early fourteenth century. The text of the triplum is full of allusions to the Old Testament, but its point is to condemn the fox (the finance minister Enguerran de Maringny) who has been devouring the chickens (the French people) while the old lion (King Philip IV) turns a blind eye. The opening text of the motetus, likewise showing the learning of the creator, is drawn from *Metamorphoses* by the ancient Roman poet Ovid, and speaks of bodies being changed into new forms—in the *Roman de Fauvel* the body politic has been turned into an ass.

Complexity, too, is found in the structure of the music. The mensuration, as in the conductus *Quare fremuerunt gentes* (no. 27), is perfect prolation, imperfect time, and perfect mode, with the minim equal to the sixteenth note and the perfect long equal to the dotted half note. In addition, there is an isorhythmic plan at work (see below). The isorhythm (same rhythm) plays out in the tenor in the repeating rhythm (the talea) and the once repeating melody (color). (The Gregorian melody upon which the motet is built has never been identified, and thus it is simply called "Neuma," or phrase of notes.) Notice that the meter changes from triple to duple for five measures in the middle of each talea (mm. 3–7, 13–17, 23–27, etc.). The long is now imperfect rather than perfect, and two quarter-note groups replace three. In the original manuscript Vitry signaled this change to the performers by coloring these notes red; this modern edition signifies the red notation by placing brackets below each passage. Mixing duple and triple meters in this fashion is yet another innovation of the *Ars nova*.

Talea	I	II	III	IV	V	VI
Color	A			B		
Measure	1	11	21	31	41	51

Philippe de Vitry
Garrit Gallus/In nova fert/Neuma (c1317)
CD 1/28

Triplum

Garrit Gallus flendo dolorose	The morning cock crows, weeping dolefully
Luget quippe Gallorum concio,	As indeed does the entire French community,
Que satrape traditur dolose,	Which has been sadly betrayed
Ex cubino sedens officio.	By the power that be.
Atque vulpes, tamquam vispilio	And the fox [Marigny], like a grave robber,
In Belial vigens astucia,	Thriving with the clever tricks of Satan,
De leonis consensu proprio	Rules with the consent of the lion [Philip IV].

Monarchisat, atat angaria.   What slavery!
Rursus, ecce, Jacob familia   See once again how the family of Jacob
Pharaone altero fugatur;   Flees from yet another Pharaoh [Genesis 25–28].

Non ut olim Iude vestigia   Not as before able to follow the footsteps of Judas,

Subintrare potens, lacrimatur   The populace laments,
In deserto fame flagellatur,   Whipped by famine in the desert,
Adiutoris carens armatura.   It lacks the armor of assistance.
Quamquam clamat, tamen spoliatur,   And although it cries out, it is still abused,
Continuo forsan moritura.   And perhaps will die.
O miserum exulum vox dura!   Bitter is the voice of the miserable exiles!
O Gallorum garritus doloris,   Oh how the French crow in sadness
Cum leonis cecitas obscura   Because the blindness of the lion [Philip IV]
Fraudi paret vulpis proditoris.   Suborns the frauds of the treacherous fox
Eius fastus sustinens erroris   [Marigny], Whose pride sustains the error.
Insurgito: alias labitur   Revolt: otherwise whatever
Et labetur quod habes honoris,   You have of honor may waver and fall away,
Quod mox in facinis tardis ultoribus itur.   Soon to be turned into a crime by latter-day avengers.

Duplum

In nova fert animus mutatas   My aim is to speak of forms changed
Dicere formas.   Into other forms [Ovid, *Metamorphoses*, I,i]:
Draco nequam quam olim penitus   Satan, although once brought down
Mirabilis crucis potencia   By the miraculous power of the cross
Debellavit Michael inclitus,   Whom divine Michael slew,
Mox Absalon munitus gracia,   Again supplied by the grace of Absolom [sic]
Mox Ulixis gaudens facundia,   Again rejoicing in the eloquence of Ulysses,
Mox lupinis dentibus armatus,   Again armed with the wolf's teeth
Sub Tersitis miles milicia   A soldier in the army of Thersites
Rursus vivit in vulpem mutatus,   Again lives, now changed into a fox [Marigny],

Cauda cuius, lumine privatus   Whose tail leads the sight-deprived
Leo, vulpe imperante, paret.   Lion [Philip IV], who supports this reigning fox.

Oves suggit pullis saciatus.   Having already had his full of chickens, He sucks the sheep.

Heu! suggere non cessat et aret   Woe! He does not cease to suck and
Ad nupcias carnibus non caret.   Thirsting for a marriage, he lacks not for flesh.

Vepullis mox, ve ceco leoni!   Woe now to the chickens, woe to the blind lion!

Coram Christotandem ve draconi.   Woe to Satan, who will be brought before Christ.

Tenor

Untitled phrase of Gregorian chant

29

Anonymous

La quinte estampie real (c1320)

Almost no instrumental music was written down during the Middle Ages, and the little that was notated appears at the ends and in gaps of manuscripts of vocal music. It is likely that the instrumentalists who performed this music had not been instructed in the intricacies of modal and mensural notation that was part of the training of singers at the church schools and at the university. All instrumental music before the fifteenth century is anonymous. Instrumentalists belonged to a different, lower social stratum from the churchmen, and instruments generally were not condoned in the church. Thus these musicians tended to perform outside the church in more popular and more informal contexts. The best of the instrumentalists, were they so fortunate, were engaged at a court, where they provided music for courtly entertainments such as dancing. *La quinte estampie real* (*The Fifth Royal Estampie*) was associated with a royal court, probably that of the king of France—indeed, it appears in a manuscript called the "manuscript du roi." The symmetrical phrasing, clear-cut endings, clear modality, and catchy rhythm suggest that this piece was typical of popular dance music. This dance is likely an example of the sort of piece that medieval minstrels could improvise on the spot—there is a clear-cut formula within which the instrumentalists could expand almost at will. For whatever reason, this and a very few other "royal" dances happened to be written down. It thus represents an example of "crystallized improvisation"—we have caught a medieval instrumentalist in the act of improvising a dance. The instrument played on this recording is a shawm.

Anonymous

La quinte estampie real (c1320)

CD 1/29

30

Anonymous
Robertsbridge Codex (c1350)
Estampie

This is another anonymous dance, but one for keyboard. It appears in a mid-fourteenth-century manuscript of French origin, but it is now in London's British Library. Because the manuscript included various records concerning the Abbey of Robertsbridge in Sussex, England, it is called the Robertsbridge Codex. The Codex contains the earliest surviving keyboard music. Whereas the preceding estampie (no. 29) likely is an example of "crystallized improvisation," this estampie may have been conceived as a "composed piece"—the puncta (sections) are longer and more complex. This may be the work of a court organist trained by the church in the ways of mensural rhythm and counterpoint. But notice that the attitude about good counterpoint was very different from that which would develop later. This medieval composition is rife with parallel fifths and octaves. Yet there are also extended passages of thirds and sixths. There is no recording of this *Estampie* on the CDs. It is not a difficult piece to play, and you are encouraged to do so. A recording is found on the Thomson-Schirmer website, where the piece is played on a harpsichord.

Anonymous
Robertsbridge Codex (c1350)
Estampie
Thomson-Schirmer Website

1. overt

2. clos

Secundus Punctus

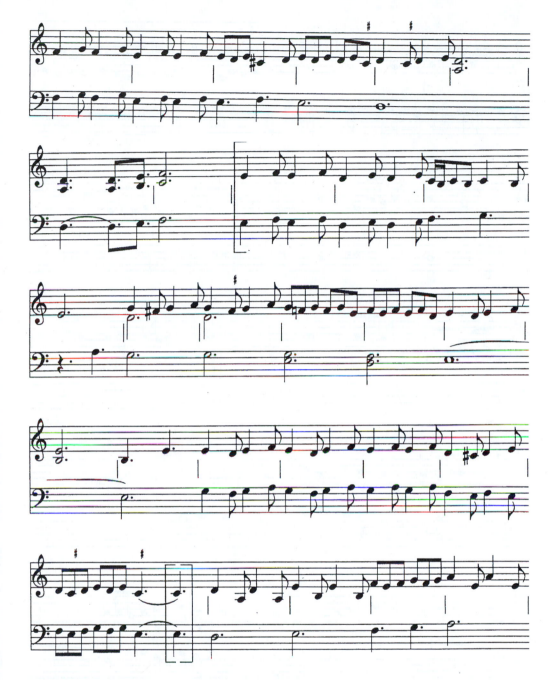

Tertius Punctus

Quartus Punctus

Chapter

12

Fourteenth-Century Music in Reims
Guillaume de Machaut

31

Guillaume de Machaut
Hoquetus David (c1364)

The *Hoquetus David* is a curious composition. It is not an instrumental dance, but neither is there a text to indicate vocal performance. Perhaps it is best to consider it as a three-voice isorhythmic motet without a text. As in many medieval compositions, number symbolism seems to be at work, specifically the number three. There are three different lines: tenor, hoquetus, and triplum (Machaut labeled the motetus part in this work the "David Hoquetus"). Using modern notation, in which measures and dotted half notes are related to Machaut's use of longs and breves (See *MWC*, Chapter 10), the composition is 123 measures (longs) in length: a number that represents counting to three: 1-2-3. Since each measure can be subdivided into three dotted half notes (Machaut's breve), there are three times more breves than longs, resulting in the number 369, the first three multiples of three (3-6-9). For composers from the *Ars antiqua* to Bach and beyond, the number three was symbolic of the Trinity. There are two talea patterns in the isorhythmic tenor. The color is stated three times in part one (**A**) and once in part two (**B**)—3:1, symbolic of the idea expressed in the Nicene Creed of the Father, Son, and Holy Ghost existing as one God. During the Middle Ages, references to the Trinity and King David abounded in the coronation service of French monarchs, and it is probable, as Machaut scholar Anne Robertson has argued, that *Hoquetus David* was written for the coronation of Charles V, which occurred on Trinity Sunday, 19 May 1364.

Needless to say, the musical technique of hocket must be pervasive in any piece that carries the name of the procedure in its title. Nearly a third of the measures in this composition include hocket. Here it is the triplum voice that is called upon to rest and then come in off the beat. While the middle part is often syncopated, it has none of the rests necessary to generate true hocket. The tenor does not actively participate in this technique. Its line is rhythmically straightforward, providing a solid foundation below. In fact, once the isorhythmic tenor proceeds eleven (**A**) or nine (**B**) bars, its rhythm is repeated. The excitement of the piece is derived from the rhythmic counterpoint between the highly predictable tenor and the wildly unpredictable triplum.

Guillaume de Machaut
Hoquetus David (c1364)
CD 2/1

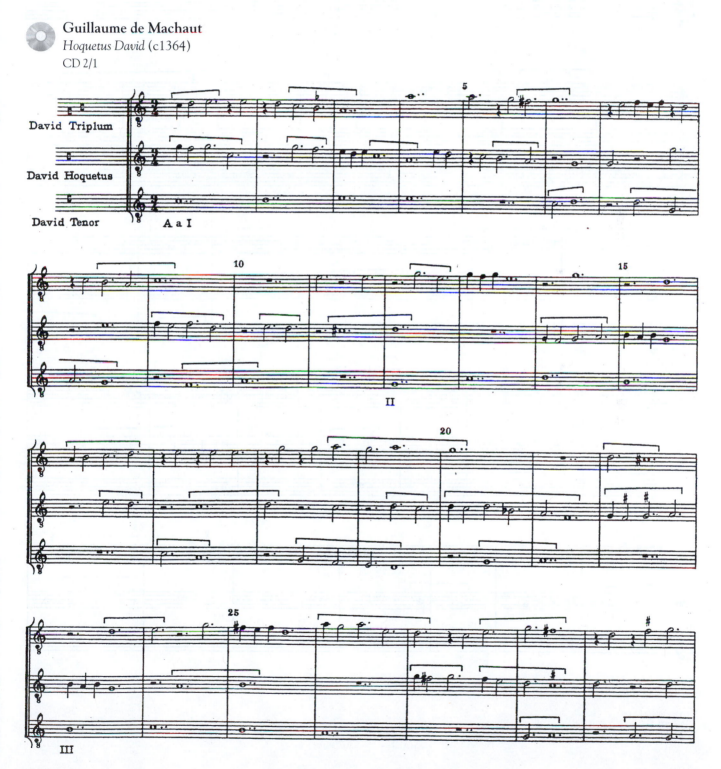

32

Guillaume de Machaut
Je puis trop bien (c1355)

Je puis trop bien recalls a tale of unrequited love drawn from the mythology of ancient Greece. In Machaut's poem, the Lover identifies with Pygmalion, the famed Greek sculptor who made an ivory statue of a woman so beautiful he fell hopelessly in love with his creation. (This story is also the basis of the Broadway musical *My Fair Lady*.) The sculptor speaks to her, caresses her, dresses her in rich robes, tucks her in at night—all in vain. Then he prays to the gods, and the statue miraculously comes to life. Machaut's Lover is not so fortunate. Nothing can soften this beauty's stone-cold demeanor. Like Pygmalion, the Lover cries out, but there is no response from the object of his affection. Machaut creates a minor masterpiece in his ballade *Je puis trop bien* by joining an image of classical beauty to an exquisitely lovely melody.

Guillaume de Machaut
Je puis trop bien (c1355)

CD 2/2

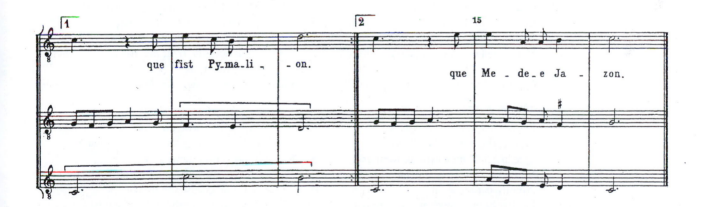

Je puis trop bien ma dame comparer	A	I can well compare my lady
A l'ymage que fist Pymalion		To the statue Pygmalion made
D'yvoire fu, tant belle et si sans per	A	Of ivory so beautiful and without equal
Que plus l'ama que Medee Jazon.		That he loved it more than Jason did Medea.
Li folz toudis la prioit,	B	Mad with love, he cried out,
Mais l'ymage re ins ne li respondoit.		But the image did not respond.
Einssi me fait celle qui mon cuer font,		Thus does she treat me, the one who melts my heart,
Qu'ades la pri et riens ne me respont.	(refrain)	*For I pray to her ever, but she does not respond.*

Second stanza

Pymalion qui mouroit pour amer	A	Pygmalion, who died for love,
Pria ses dieus par telle affection		Prayed to the gods with such passion
Que la froideur de l'ymage tourner	A	That her icy demeanor
Vit en chalour et sa dure facon		Turn to warmth, and her hard exterior
Amolir, car vie avoit	B	Soften, because she had life
Et char humeinne et doucement parloit		And human flesh, and spoke softly,
Mais ma dame de ce trop mi confont		But my lady in all this confounds me
Qu'ades la pri et riens ne me respont.	(refrain)	*For I pray to her ever, but she does not respond.*

Third stanza

Or weille Amours le dur en dous muer	A	Now I wish Love to change the hard to soft
De celle a qui j'ay fait de mon cuer don,		Of her to whom I have given my heart,
Et son froit cuer de m'amour aviver,	A	And liven her cold heart with my love,
Si que de li puisse avoir guerredon.		And thus have recompense from her.
Mais Amour en li conjoit	B	But Love is pleased to see in her
Un fier desdaing, et le grant desir voyt		A proud disdain, and he sees the great desire
Qui m'ocirra; si croi que cil troy font		Which will kill me; these three are the cause
Qu'ades la pri et riens ne me respont.	(refrain)	*For I pray to her ever, but she does not respond.*

33

Guillaume de Machaut
Douce dame jolie (before 1350)

The virelai, one of the *formes fixes*, developed out of a dance form that was sung rather than played on instruments. A chorus would have sung the refrain and a soloist would have executed the new verses of text. Thus in the form **AbbaA**, the chorus would have sung the **A** (the first section with the text refrain). When successive strophes were strung together, the form **AbbaAbbaAbbaA** resulted. The issue of the origins of the virelai in dance clouds the question of how a piece like Machaut's *Douce dame jolie* (*Fair sweet lady*) should be sung. Should it be executed as a solo song in a gentle lyrical manner? Or should it be truer to its roots and project a lively dance-like aura? The recording follows the former approach.

Guillaume de Machaut

Douce dame jolie (before 1350)

CD 2/3

Douce dame jolie,	A	Fair sweet lady
Pour Dieu ne pensés mie		for God's sake never think
Que neulle ait signourie		that any woman rules
Seur moy, fors vous seulement.		my heart, except you alone.
Qu'adès sans tricherie, chierie	b	I have cherished you long
Vous ay, et humblement		and served you faithfully
Tous les jours de ma vie servie	b	All the days of my life
Sans vilein pensement.		without a base thought.
Helas! Et je mendie	a	Alas! I must do without
D'esperance et d'aïe,		hope and help, and thus
Dont ma joie est fenie,		my joy has ended,
Se pité ne vous en prent.		unless you pity me.
Douce dame jolie . . . (refrain)	A	Fair sweet lady . . .
Mais vo douce maistrie, maistrie	b	But your sweet mastery masters
Mon cuer si durement		my heart so harshly
Qu'elle le contralie et lie	b	That it confounds it, and binds it
En amours, tellement		in love, so much so

Qu'il n'a de riens envie	a	That it desires nothing	
Fors d'estre en vo baillie		but to be in your power;	
Et se ne li ottrie		and yet your heart grants	
Vos cuers nul aligement.		no relief.	
Douce dame jolie . . . (refrain)	A	*Fair sweet lady . . .*	

Et quant ma maladie, garie	b	And because my malady	
Ne sera nullement		in no way will be cured	
Sans vous, douce anemie, qui lie	b	Without you, sweet enemy, who rejoices	
Estes de mon tourment		at my torment,	
A jointes mains deprie	a	With hands joined I pray	
Vo cuer, puis qu'il m'oublie		your heart, since it has forgotten me,	
Que temprement m'ocie,		soon kill me	
Car trop langui longuement.		for I have languished too long.	
Douce dame jolie . . . (refrain)	A	*Fair sweet lady . . .*	

34

Guillaume de Machaut
Kyrie of the *Mass of Our Lady* (c1360)

In many ways, Machaut's *Messe de Nostre Dame* is the most significant composition found in all early music. Not only is it the longest piece of polyphonic music from the Middle Ages, it is also the first unified Mass cycle to come down to us. Fifty years before it became a common practice during the Renaissance, Machaut set all the sections of the Ordinary of the Mass as a single work. While he wrote a setting for the sixth movement of the Ordinary, the *Ite missa est*, later composers did not follow his example, and it became standard to set only the first five parts of the Ordinary. Machaut unified his composition on a variety of levels, only a few of which are mentioned here. There is a liturgical unity: the chants that form the basis of the tenor line in each movement were derived from liturgies devoted to "Our Lady," the Virgin Mary. There is musical unity: the use of isorhythm in five of the movements, and a distinctive descending motive that is common to them all. In the *Kyrie* movement, this motive is most prominent in the "Christe" section, where it appears many times and in more than one voice.

Another feature that sets this Mass apart from earlier compositions is vocal sonority. Unlike polyphony from the *Ars antiqua* and even the motets of Philippe de Vitry, where all the voices share the same basic range and tessitura, Machaut distributes the four choral parts into distinctive high and low ranges. What is more, there is a purpose to this expansion of the musical texture, beyond the obvious broadening of the texture—each voice now plays a specific role within a specific range. The tenor and contratenor combine to establish a consistent harmonic foundation. For the isorhythmic tenor line, Machaut used the well-known chant melody *Kyrie, Omnipotens genitor* as the color (see no. 11) and added a talea pattern to suit the required length of each section. Because the contratenor works in tandem with the tenor line so that the cadences consistently fall on D, these two voices must have been composed as a single process. The two upper voices also have distinctive characteristics. The motetus line has a wide range and moves with more leaps; its function is more akin to harmonic filler. The triplum, with its narrow range and more conjunct movement, has a more melodic role.

Finally, recall that every *Kyrie* is comprised of a threefold petition: "Kyrie eleison" (three times), "Christe eleison" (three times), and "Kyrie eleison" (three times). When Machaut composed his *Kyrie*, he wrote only four polyphonic sections: one for each of the threefold repetitions and a more elaborate version for the ninth statement. To perform this movement, the musicians must either repeat the polyphony or alternate it with monophonic chant, as is the practice in the recording.

Guillaume de Machaut
Kyrie of the *Mass of Our Lady* (c1360)
CD 2/4

three times

three times

107

e - ley - son.

e - ley - sor.

e - - ley - - - son.

e - - ley - - son.

Ky - ri - e

Ky - ri - e

Ky - - - ri - e

I

Ky - ri - - - e

I

II

II

Kyrie eleison.	Lord, have mercy upon me.
Christe eleison.	Christ, have mercy upon me.
Kyrie eleison.	Lord, have mercy upon me.

Chapter 13

Avignon, Symbolic Scores, and the *Ars Subtilior*

35

Baude Cordier
Tout par compas suy composés (c1391)

When we come to the music of the late fourteenth century, we are faced with something akin to an explosion of rhythmic complexity—musicians explored sophisticated and minute relationships between durations, and it seems they pursued these experiments with wild abandon. Syncopations, polymeters, and intricate rhythmic patterns abound. This highly complex musical style is called the *Ars subtilior,* and rarely has there been more rhythmic complexity than in this repertory. Some have even speculated that the most extreme examples of the *Ars subtilior* were merely intellectual exercises, and never meant to be performed. To be sure, this is difficult music—for performers and editors, as well.

Baude Cordier's *Tout par compas suy composés* is a fascinating piece not only because of the symbolic way in which it is notated (see MWC, Fig. 13-3) but also because of its complex rhythmic relationships. It is so complicated, in fact, that there are several different editions of the work—so far, no two scholars can agree in print as to exactly how long certain notes are to be held or when the repeats required by the rondeau form should begin. Similarly, no recording of quality agrees with any of the published modern editions. As a result, when you listen to this recording there will be moments during which the musical performance will not agree with the score, especially with respect to repetitions. This is one of those instances in which medieval music eludes our attempts to capture it in all of its particulars.

Baude Cordier
Tout par compas suy composés (c1391)
CD 2/5

Tenor cuius finis est 2a. nota.

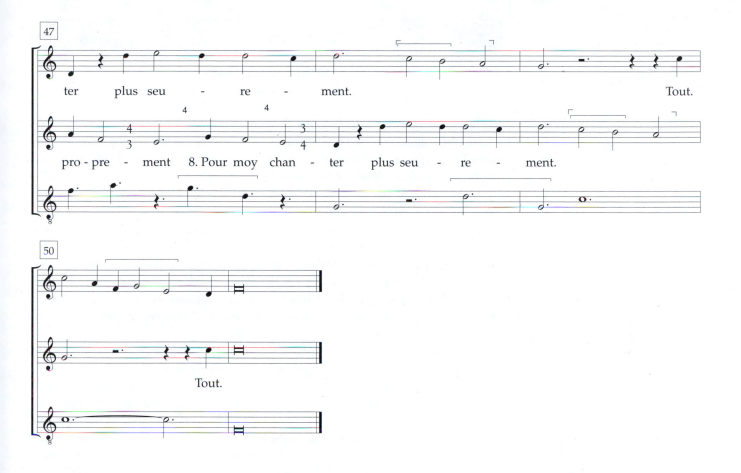

Tout par compas suy composés   A(1)   *All with a compass am I composed*
En ceste rode proprement   *Properly, as befits a round*
Pour moy chanter plus seurement. B   *To sing me more surely.*
Regarde com suy disposés   a   Look how I am disposed,
Compaing, je te pri chierement.   Companion, I pray you kindly.
Tout par compas suy composés   A   *All with a compass am I composed*
En ceste rode proprement.   *Properly, as befits a round.*
Trois temps entiers par toy posés a(2)   Three times you go around me entirely
Chacer me pues joyeusement   You can chase me joyfully,
S'en chantant as vray sentiment. b   If in singing you're true to me.
Tout par compas suy composés   A(3)   *All with a compass am I composed*
En ceste rode proprement   *Properly, as befits a round*
Pour moy chanter plus seurement. B   *To sing me more surely.*

Score courtesy of Alexander Blachly.

36

Philippus de Caserta
Par les bons Gedeons (c1385)

In Caserta's *Par les bons Gedeons*, the rhythmic wanderings of the cantus are kept on course not only by the solid framework of the lower voices but also by a rigid formal plan. The poem is a ballade set to a clear **AAB** musical structure. Each of the two stanzas ends with a refrain accompanied by what might be called "musical rhyme"—the music heard at the close of section **A** returns at the end of section **B**. The text also has its own refrain, which reads "Par le souverayne pape qui s'apelle Clement" ("By the sovereign pope who is called Clement"), which confirms that Philippus de Caserta composed this ballade to honor Clement VII (1378–1394). Indeed, the piece is a spirited defense of the Avignonese pope during the Great Schism. Clement is a hero of biblical proportions. Just as the warrior Gideon and the mighty Samson rescued God's chosen people of Israel, so Pope Clement will save the Christian world, removing the "anger, division, and partiality" that accompany the Great Schism.

As a theorist, Philippus de Caserta wrote one of the first descriptions of syncopation, and the score of this ballade illustrates the heavy syncopation that exists between the cantus and the lower two voices. The bracketed notes above the cantus show how we would perceive the line if it were heard in isolation. Yet when sung against the rhythmic regularity of the bottom two lines, it provides a rhythmic battle that mirrors the spiritual warfare described in the text. Philippus was also interested in developing a notational system that permitted more varied metrical structures than the four introduced in de Vitry's treatise, the *Ars nova* (see MWC, page 94). We see one such example in this ballade. The meter has been consistently subdividing the breve (half-note) into two semi-breves (quarter-notes), but suddenly in measure 29 an extra semibreve is added. We cannot say inserted into the "measure," because there were no actual measures or bar lines written into the music of that time. Bar lines do not become widespread in music until the seventeenth century.

Philippus de Caserta
Par les bons Gedeons (c1385)
CD 2/6

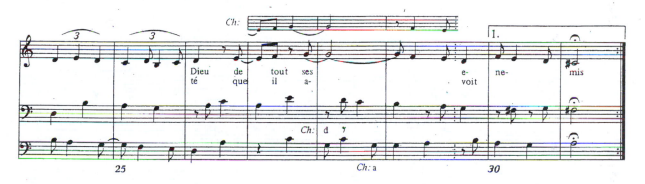

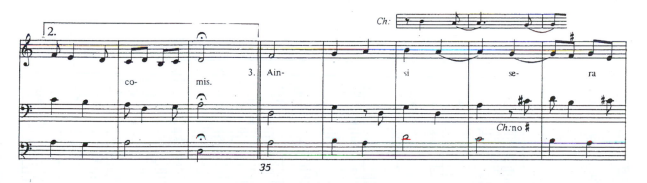

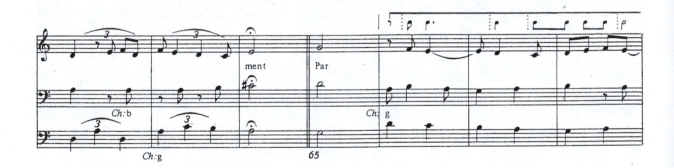

Par les bons Gedeons et Sanson delivré	A	By the good Gideon and Samson were delivered
Fu le peuple de Dieu de tous ses enemis		The people of God from all their enemies.
De mourtel servitud' auquel estoit livré	A	From the mortal servitude in which they dwelled
Pour la iniquité que il avoit comis.		Owing to the sins they had committed.
Ainsi sera le monde de bas en haut remis	B	Thus shall the world be restored, bottom to top,
En la sainte vertu de celi qui ne ment		By the saintly virtue of him who lieth not
Par le souverayne pape qui s'apelle Clement.		*By the sovereign pope whose name is Clement.*

Ire, devision et partialité	A	Anger, division, and partiality,
Inordiné desir desus orgueil assis		Excessive desire supported by pride
Sunt cause de la sisme per quoy humilité	A	Are the cause of Schism, in which humility,
Union, karaté et la foy sont jus mis.		Union, charity, and faith are put in doubt.
Le mondes est jus mis, se Diex par sum avis	B	The world is put is doubt, if God in his wisdom
Ne le remet en vie de vray sentiment		Does not restore it to a life of true understanding
Par le souverayne pape qui s'apelle Clement.		*By the sovereign pope whose name is Clement.*

Part

II

THE LATE MIDDLE AGES
AND EARLY RENAISSANCE

Chapter 14

From the Late Middle Ages to the Early Renaissance

37

Jacopo da Bologna
Non al suo amante (c1350)

Why does a composer named Jacopo da Bologna (c1310–1386) appear in a discussion of music of Florence? Jacopo was apparently born in Bologna, well north of Florence, and worked for a time in the northern Italian cities of Verona and Milan—these are the few shards of his biography as we know it. Yet, it is just possible that this composer did, in fact, end his days in Florence, for a "Jachopo da Bolongnia" is listed as a member of an important confraternity in Florence during the 1370s. Certainly Jacopo's music was well known to the Florentines. The Squarcialupi Codex contains some twenty-eight pieces by him, almost all of this composer's thirty-four surviving works. Of these thirty-four pieces, thirty-two are madrigals.

As with most trecento madrigals, the form of Jacopo's *Non al suo amante* is **AAB**, the same as is found in the French ballade established by Guillaume de Machaut and other creators of early French secular song. Jacopo's madrigal sets a poem by the famous humanist poet Francesco Petrarch. Typical of the Renaissance humanists, Petrarch includes an allusion to classical mythology, specifically to Diana, the Roman goddess of the hunt and of chastity.

The Romans viewed Diana as the embodiment of modesty. One day the unfortunate hunter Actaeon accidentally saw her bathing nude in cool waters. So infuriated was the goddess that she changed Actaeon into a stag, and his own dogs devoured him. In Jacopo's madrigal, the object of the lover's desire is as chaste and unresponsive as the goddess Diana. Fortunately for this lover, he suffers only a chill. In Jacopo's music the momentary effect of the "chill of love" is conveyed by a change from duple to triple meter.

Jacopo da Bologna
Non al suo amante (c1350)
CD 2/7

Non al suo amante più Diana piacque	a	Not did Diana ever more please her lover
Quando per tal ventura tutta ignuda		As when, through good fortune,
La vidi in mezzo de le gelide acque.		He saw her naked in the midst of the cool waters.
Ch'a me la pastorell'alpestra e cruda	a	As did please me the cruel shepherdess,
Posta a bagnar un leggiadretretto velo		Washing her white veil, which protects
Ch'a l'aura il vago e biondo capel chiuda.		Her fine blond hair from blowing free.

Ritornello

Tal che mi fece quand'egli arde 'l cielo,	b	So that it made me, now when the sky is fiery,
Tutto tremar d'un amoroso gielo.		All tremble with the chill of love.

The text in the translation is the one originally written by Petrarch, whereas that appearing in the score is derived from textually less accurate musical sources.

38

Francesco Landini
Or su, gentili spirti (c1389)

Francesco Landini (c1325–1397), blind organist of Florence, was the most renowned composer of the trecento. Numerous contemporaries praised his erudition in matters of philosophy, poetry, and politics, as well as music. Surviving under Landini's name are 154 compositions, including 140 ballatas. A vivid portrait of the composer is offered in Giovanni da Prato's narrative poem *Il Paradiso* (1389), in which Landini takes part in discussions of the pressing political and moral issues of the day. Music played an important role in the social gatherings of the sort described in *Il Paradiso*, and da Prato's poem offers an account of a performance of Landini's three-voice ballata *Or su, gentili spirti*. Two ladies sang the ballata, accompanied by a gentleman. Yet da Prato's literary report presents a special challenge to the musicologist of today when constructing a modern edition of the piece.

Or su, gentili spirti survives in only one manuscript, the Squarcialupi Codex. Only part of the text (sections 1, 2, and 5) is written beneath the cantus in this manuscript, but the residual text (sections 3 and 4) is given at the end of the ballata. It is the job of the editor to place these lines of poetry beneath the music of this top part. More challenging still, the literary account says that the second voice, labeled "contratenor," was sung by a woman, presumably an alto; yet no text whatsoever appears beneath that voice part in the original manuscript. Again, it is the job of the musicologist, drawing upon the text supplied for the cantus voice, to situate the text below the music of the contratenor. Finally, the tessitura of the contratenor part, as written in the Squarcialupi Codex, is too low for a female voice, and thus the editor must transpose the ballata upward into a range that is comfortable for female singers. The recording of *Or su, gentili spirti*, conforming to the description of the performance recounted in da Prato's *Il Paradiso*, was made especially to accompany this anthology. It is the first recording of this lovely ballata.

Francesco Landini

Or su, gentili spirti (c1389)

CD 2/8

*All parts transposed up a fifth from original pitch.

*These five notes are a step lower in the original.

(ripresa) Or su, gentili spirti, ad amar pronti,	**A** Come now, gentle spirits, ready to love,
Volete voi vederc 'l Paradiso?	Do you want to see Paradise?
Mirate d'esta petra 'l vago viso.	Admire the beautiful face of this [precious] stone.
(piede) Nelle sue luce sancte ard' e sfavilla	**b** Victorious love burns and glows
Amor victorioso, che divampa	In her holy eyes, which inflames he who
Per dolcezza di gloria chi la mira	Gazes upon her through the sweetness of glory.
(piede) Ma l'alma mia, fedelissima ancilla	**b** But my soul, most faithful helpmate,
Piatà non trova in questa chiara lampa	Finds no pity in this clear light,
E null'altro che lei ama o disira.	Nor does it love or desire anything else than her.
(volta) O sacra iddea, al tuo servo un po' spira	**a** O holy image, to your servant show some
Mercé; mercé sol chiamo, già conquiso:	Mercy; already conquered, mercy I alone ask:
Dé, fallo pria che morte m'abbia anciso.	Come, do this before death kills me.
(ripresa) Or su, gentili spirti . . .	**A** Come now, gentle spirits . . .

Music at the Cathedral of Florence

Chapter 15

39

Guillaume Dufay
Nuper rosarum flores (1436)

Guillaume Dufay's *Nuper rosarum flores* (*Recently Roses*) is a grand isorhythmic motet commissioned to make even more splendid one of the glorious occasions in the history of Florence: the dedication on 25 March 1436 of the gigantic dome that crowned the city's cathedral. Pope Eugenius IV, then residing in Florence, arrived at the church on that day by means of a specially constructed, elevated walkway nearly a mile in length. He was greeted at the door by the clergy of the cathedral and the singers of his private chapel, then under the direction of Dufay. Surely among the first musical sounds to reach the pontiff's ears were those of Dufay's motet, for it was built on the chant for the Introit, the opening portion of the Mass. The various musical proportions of the motet, and their meaning, are discussed in detail in *MWC* (Chapter 15). In brief, the numbers 2, 4, 7, 14, and 28, as well as the proportion 6:4:2:3, lie at the heart of the work's musical and textual structure. Perhaps not to be outdone by a musician, the ecclesiastical and civic authorities of Florence also engaged in their own bit of number symbolism that day, as a contemporary chronicler reports: "After Mass the pope gave the benediction to the populace and granted indulgences to all in said church of seven years and seven forty days . . . and the esteemed town council of Florence handed over to the pope fourteen condemned prisoners." Whether the general populace was attuned to all this religious, civic, and musical symbolism cannot be known. The listener of today may experience the work, not on the level of its large-scale proportions, but rather at that of the rapidly moving quarter notes. The duration of the quarter note remains constant in all four sections of the motet, which tends to obscure the symbolic relationship of the four sections (6:4:2:3).

Guillaume Dufay
Nuper rosarum flores (1436)
CD 2/9

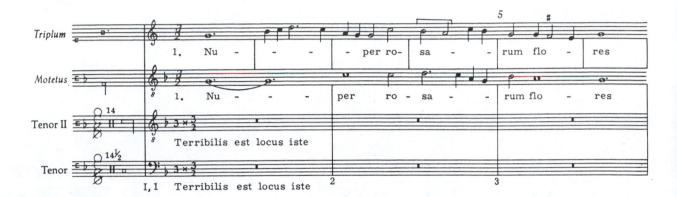

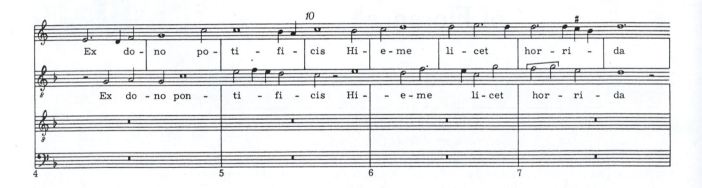

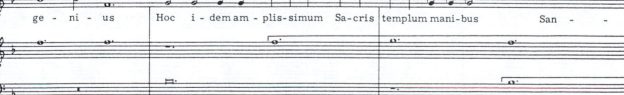

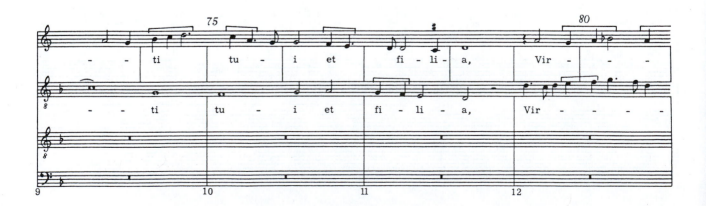

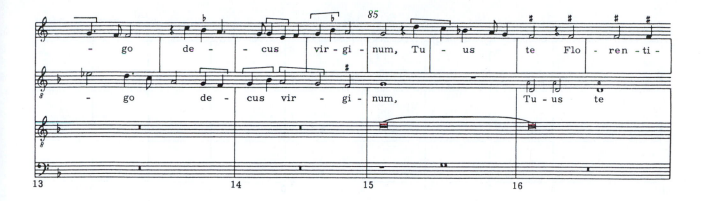

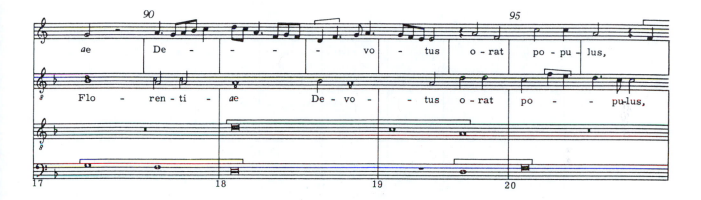

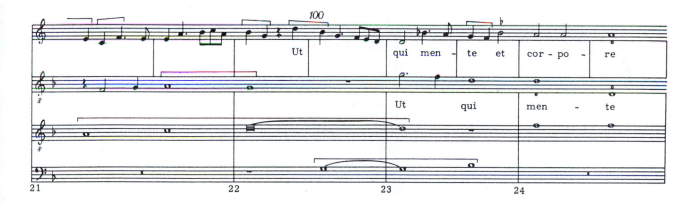

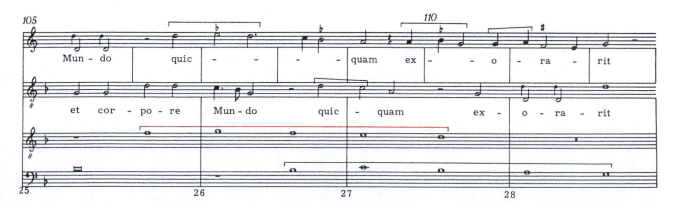

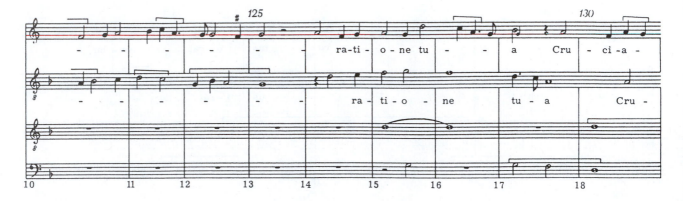

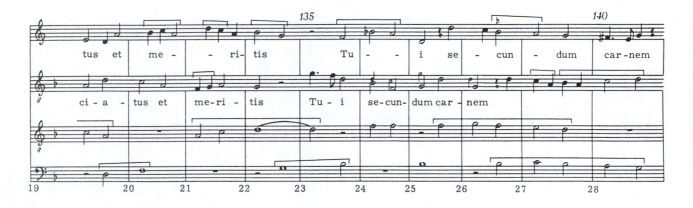

Nuper rosarum flores	Recently roses given by the pope
Ex dono pontificis	Have not ceased to adorn,
Hieme licet horrida	Cruel winter having passed,
Tibi, virgo celica,	The Temple,
Pie et sancte deditum	Majestic in its engineering,
Grandis templum machinae	Dedicated to the Virgin
Condecorarunt perpetim.	In piety and holiness.

Hodie vicarius	Today the vicar
Jesu Christi et Petri	Of Jesus Christ and successor
Successor Eugenius	Of Peter, Eugenius,
Hoc idem amplissimum	This same most enormous Temple
Sacris templum manibus	With sacred hands
Sanctisque liquoribus	And holy oils
Consecrare dignatus est.	Has deigned to consecrate.

Igitur, alma parens	Therefore, sweet parent
Nati tui et filia	And daughter of your son,
Virgo decus virginum,	God, virgin of virgins,
Tuus te Florentiae	To you your devoted
Devotus orat populus	Populace of Florence petitions
It qui mente et corpore	So that whoever begs for something
Mundo quicquam exorarit,	With pure spirit and body,

Oratione tua	May, by your prayers
Cruciatus et meritis	And the merits
Tui secundum carnem	Owing to His carnal torment,
Nati domini sui	Of your son, their lord,
Grata beneficia	Be worthy to receive
Veniamque reatum	Gracious benefits and
Accipere mereatur.	Forgiveness of sins.
Amen.	Amen.

Music in England

Chapter 16

40

Anonymous
Sumer is icumen in (c1300)

The Summer Canon is one of the most famous pieces in English cultural history and certainly one of the most important in the history of music: it is both the first six-voice composition and the earliest round to survive. Musicologists argue over its date; some say it is as early as 1250, others as late as 1325. Arguing for the earlier date is the rudimentary nature of the rhythm, which harkens back to the rhythmic modes of the time of Leoninus and Perotinus (c1200). Perhaps supporting the later date is the large number of voices (six) involved. The English text is a hymn to the never-ending process of birth and regeneration associated with spring. The Latin text, which alludes to Christ's rescue of faithful souls in Purgatory at the time of the resurrection, can be read as a paean to spring as well, being theologically relevant to Easter and the rebirth of the soul. In addition, the notes of the pes (lower two voices) are the first notes of the chant *Regina caeli*, which was sung at Compline from Easter to Pentecost.

So deeply ingrained was the Summer Canon in the collective psyche of the English—and Anglophiles generally—that in 1902 the seventeen-year-old American poet Ezra Pound (1885–1972) wrote a parody of the text. Entitled *Ancient Music*, it begins "Winter is icummen in," and goes on to lament the season's miserable weather.

As to the musical structure of the Summer Canon: together the four-voice canon and the two-voice pes create a succession of alternating D-major, E-minor triads, as we would call them. Canons are often constructed around just one or two chords, because it makes the process of writing a canon easier. In the original notation the chords were F major and G minor; the piece has been transposed here to make it easier to sing. Try it! (Audio for this piece is found on the Thomson-Schirmer Website.)

Sumer is icumen in,	Summer is coming in,
Lhude sing cuccu!	Loudly sing, cuckoo!
Growedth sed and bloweth med	Seeds sprout and the meadow blooms,
And springth the wde nu.	And new wood growth appears.
Sing cuccu!	Sing cuckoo!
Awe bleteth after lomb,	Ewe bleats after lamb,
Lhouth after calve cu.	Cow lows after calf,
Bulluc sterteth, bucke verteth,	Bullock leaps, he-goat farts,
Murie sing cuccu!	Merrily sing cuckoo!
Wel singes thu cuccu.	Well sing you cuckoo.
Ne swik thu naver nu!	Don't ever stop!
Perspice Christicola,	Observe, worshippers of Christ,
que dignatio!	what gracious condescension!

Celicus agricola   How the heavenly husbandman
pro vitis vicio,   for the sin of the vine [in Eden]
filio   not sparing his son
non parcens exposuit   exposed him
mortis exicio.   to the pains of death.
Qui captivos semivivos   Those half-dead captives
a supplicio   sentenced [to Purgatory];
vite donat   he restores to life
et secum coronat   and crowns them next to him
in celi solio.   on the heavenly throne.

Pes: Sing cuccu!   Sing, cuckoo!

Anonymous
Sumer is icumen in (c1300)
Thomson-Schirmer Website

41

Anonymous
Agincourt Carol (c1420)

Of the more than 120 English carols from the fifteenth century, the majority are about Christmas, while only a few are about Easter or other topics. Almost all of these carols feature a tuneful style, triple meter, and English discant (the prominent use of euphonious chords with thirds and sixths). Moreover, the vast majority of these English holiday carols employ a form called strophe and burden (refrain). Soloists likely sang the successive strophes, and a chorus took charge in the burden. Often the burden consists not of English words, but rather of simple, well-known Latin exclamations such as "Gloria in excelsis" ("Glory to God in the highest") or "Christus natus hodie" ("Christ is born today").

The Agincourt Carol is not a religious carol but a political one, for it celebrates the great victory of the English king Henry V over the French at the Battle of Agincourt (1415) during the Hundred Years' War. Here the various strophes tell the story of Henry's victory, while the choral burden asks that all England render thanks to God: "Deo gratias, Anglia, redde pro victoria." Sometimes the music proceeds directly in 6/3 chords through short (usually four-bar) phrases, and sometimes this chordal framework is energized with light counterpoint.

Anonymous
Agincourt Carol (c1420)
CD 2/10

Owre Kynge went forth to Normandy
With grace and might of chivalry
Ther God for hym wrought mervelusly;
Wherfore Englonde may call and cry. Deo gratias.
Burden II: (three voices)
Deo gratias, Anglia, redde pro Victoria!

He sette a sege, forsothe to say,
To Harflu towne with ryal array;
That toune he wan and made affray
That Fraunce shal rewe tyl domesday. Deo gratias.
Burden II: Deo gratias . . .

Then went hym forth, owre king comely,
In Agincourt feld he faught manly;
Thorw grace of God most marvelously,
He had both feld and victory. Deo gratias.
Burden II: Deo gratias . . .

Ther lordys, erles and barone
Were slayne and taken and that full soon,
And summe were broght into Lundone
With joye and blisse and gret renone. Deo Gratias.
Burden II: Deo gratias . . .

Almighty God he keep owre kynge,
His peple, and alle his well-wyllynge,
And give them grace wythoute ending;
Then may we call and savely syng: Deo gratias.
Burden II: Deo gratias . . .

140

42

John Dunstaple
Quam pulcra es (c1420)

John Dunstaple (c1390–1453) was the most esteemed English composer of the early fifteenth century—at least far more surviving pieces carry his name (about 60) than that of any other English composer of this period. Judging from the epitaph on his tombstone, Dunstaple was a mathematician and astronomer, as well as a musician. Today college libraries in Cambridge and Oxford preserve treatises by Dunstaple filled with astronomical drawings and calculations. This fact suggests that Dunstaple was very much a man of the Middle Ages, a time when music and the sciences were closely linked. Yet in matters of music, Dunstaple showed himself to be a composer of the emerging Renaissance. The sonorities that he constructs make abundant use of thirds and sixths, and his writing is almost entirely free of musical dissonance (seconds, sevenths, and tritones). Indeed, Dunstaple's motet *Quam pulcra es* is so dissonance-free that it can be called a pan-consonant motet. The only moments of dissonance (other than those resulting from passing eighth-notes) occur in measures 21, 38, and 52, where a seventh sounds on a strong beat. But these moments are carefully prepared and quickly resolved, providing an early example of what we would call a 7–6 suspension. Notice, finally, that in measures 12–14 the music proceeds almost entirely in parallel 6/3 chords, a sure sign of the influence of the improvisatory technique of English faburden.

John Dunstaple
Quam pulcra es (c1420)
CD 2/11

Quam pulcra es et quam decora,
Carissima in deliciis.
Statura tua assimilata est palme
Et ubera tua botris.
Caput tuum ut Carmelus,
Collum tuum sicut turris eburnea
Veni, dilecte mi,
Egrediamur in agrum, et videamus
Si flores fructus parturierunt
Si floruerunt mala punica.
Ibi dabo tibi ubera mea.
Alleluia.

How beautiful thou art, and fair,
My beloved, in thy delights.
Thy stature is like a palm tree,
And thy breasts like unto round grapes.
Thy head is like Mount Carmel and
Thy neck like a tower of ivory.
Oh come, my beloved;
Let us go into the fields and see
If the blossoms have borne fruit,
If the pomegranates have flowered.
There I will give to you my breasts.
Alleluia.

Music at the Court of Burgundy

43

Gilles Binchois
Dueil angoisseus (c1435)

Gilles Binchois (c1400–1460) was an ordained priest who left us more than sixty settings of sacred texts, including individual Mass movements, Magnificats, and motets. However, this musical priest passed his professional days not in a monastery or cathedral, but rather at the very worldly court of the dukes of Burgundy, where he served as singer and composer in the ducal chapel. It was in the context of courtly life that Binchois created his nearly sixty secular songs, and in these we approach the essence of the Burgundian chanson. Binchois' chansons are lyrical songs in miniature, usually consisting of no more than a minute or so of musical material; they achieve longer duration (three to five minutes) only because the *formes fixes* require frequent sectional repetition. Binchois' *Dueil angoisseus* sets an extraordinary text by Burgundian poet Christine de Pisan, in which she laments the unexpected loss of her husband.

The piece progresses through the careful shaping of a haunting melody line in phrases of five, six, or seven bars, each carrying a separate syntactical unit of the text. Both **A** and **B** sections, however, begin with a short exclamation of only four syllables, and both are only three bars in length. *Dueil angoisseus* demonstrates a clear sense of mode (Lydian with B♭), and the first and second endings (bar 15) can be thought of, in modern terms, as ending on a half cadence, and then a full cadence. The essential structural parts are the cantus (melody) and supporting tenor, with the contratenor providing harmonic filler.

This chanson survives in three somewhat different versions (two for three voices, but with different contratenors, and one for four voices with two contratenors). A three-voice version chosen from a manuscript from the Burgundian court is provided here.

Gilles Binchois
Dueil angoisseus (c1435)
CD 2/12

1) Fehlt im Ms., ergänzt nach *Esc B.*

Dueil angoisseus, rage demesuree,	A	Anguished mourning, immeasurable rage,
Grief, desespoir plain de forsennement,		Grief, despair full of madness,
Langor sans fin et vie maleuree,	A	Languor without end, a life accursed,
Plaine de plour, d'angoisee et de tourment.		Full of lamentation, anguish, and torment.
Coeur doloreux qui vit obscurement,	B	A dolorous heart which lives in darkness,
Tenebreux corps sur le point de partir,		A shadowy corpse on the point of death,
Ay sans cesser continuellement,		These have I without cessation,
Et si ne puis ne garir ne morir.		*And so can neither recover nor die.*

44

Guillaume Dufay
Lamentatio sanctae Matris Ecclesiae Constantinopolitanae (1454)

Guillaume Dufay was a remarkably versatile individual. He held a degree in canon law, wrote poetry, composed more than two hundred musical works, both polyphonic and monophonic, served as a church administrator, and at one point (1438–1439) was an ambassador to a pan-European church council. Dufay's musical *oeuvre* is equally diversified, including secular songs in both French and Italian, monophonic "Gregorian" chants, small-scale liturgical pieces, old-style isorhythmic motets (see no. 39), and newer-style cantus firmus Masses (see no. 45). Because he was both a musician and a witness to some of the major political events of the day, it is not surprising that a few of Dufay's musical compositions took notice of these events, just as his motet *Nuper rosarum flores* (no. 39) marked an important moment in the history of church architecture.

Perhaps no political event of the mid fifteenth century was more momentous for the West than the fall of Constantinople (the center of the Eastern Christian Church) to the armies of the Moslems on 29 May 1453. Dufay composed four laments to mourn this loss, though only one survives: *Lamentatio sanctae Matris Ecclesiae Constantinopolitanae* (*Lament for the Holy Mother Church of Constantinople*). Dufay's lamentation is a motet-chanson (a combination of the two genres), with a French text in the upper voice and a Latin chant in the tenor. The tenor quotes a phrase of plainsong (*Omnes amici ejus*) for Good Friday that sets a section of the Lamentations of Jeremiah—just as Jeremiah laments the fall of Jerusalem for the Jews, so Dufay's motet-chanson laments the loss of Constantinople for Christians.

The upper voice, by contrast, is crafted in the form of a secular French song in which the figure of the Holy Mother Church sings before God for redress. The poignant song in the cantus and the ancient wail of Jeremiah in the tenor combine to form an especially moving plea.

Guillaume Dufay
Lamentatio sanctae Matris Ecclesiae Constantinopolitanae (1454)
CD 2/13

tel - le dur - te vil - lai - - ne Fai - re a mon filz, qui

QUI CON - SO - LE - TUR E - AM EX O - - MNI - BUS

tant m'a hou - nou - re - - - - - e.

CA - - RIS E - - JUS.

C

Dont suis de bien et de joy - e se - pa - re - e, Sans qui vi - vant veul - le

Dont suis de bien

Dont suis de bien

en - ten - dre mes plains. A toy, seul dieu,

II

O - MNES A -

du for - fait me com - - - plains, Du gref tourment et dou - lou - reulx

MI - CI E - JUS SPRE - VE - RUNT E - AM.

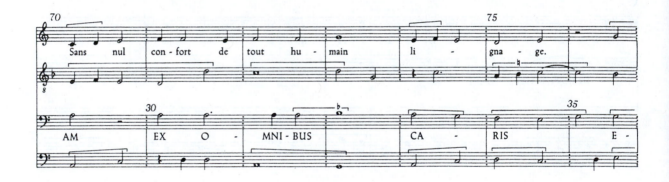

D

- oul - tra - ge, Que voy souf - frir au plus bel des hu - mains

NON EST QUI CON - SO - LE - TUR E - -

Sans nul con - fort de tout hu - main li - gna - ge.

AM EX O - MNI - BUS CA - RIS E -

- JUS.

Triplum (Virgin Mary):

O tres piteulx de tout espoir fontaine,
Pere du filz dont suis mere esploree,

Plaindre me viens a ta court souveraine.
De ta puissance et de nature humaine,
Qui ont souffert telle durte villaine
Faire a mon filz, qui tant m'a hounouree.

Tenor (Israel):

Omnes amici ejus spreverunt eam.
Non est qui consoletur eam
Ex omnibus caris ejus.

Triplum (Virgin Mary):

Dont suis de bien et de joye separee,
Sans qui vivant veulle entendre mes plains.
A toy, seul dieu, du forfait me complains,
Du gref tourment et douloureulx oultrage.
Que moy souffrir au plus bel des humains,
Sans nul confort de tout humain lignage.

Tenor (Israel):

Omnes amici ejus spreverunt eam . . .

O most merciful fountain of all hope,
Father of the son of whom I am the
    despairing mother,
I come to your sovereign court,
To appeal to your power and human kindness
For those who have done such villainy
To my son, who has done me such honor.

All her friends have deserted her.
Among all those dear to her
There are none to console her.

Thus I am separated from goodness and joy
And not a living soul will heed my pleas.
To you, sole God, I bring my complaint,
Of grievous suffering and pain
That the finest of men suffers
Without humans offering any comfort.

All her friends have deserted her . . .

45

Guillaume Dufay
a. Tune: *L'Homme armé* (c1460)
b. *Kyrie* of the *Missa L'Homme armé* (c1460)

The capture of Constantinople emboldened the Moslems and their leader Sultan Mehmet II (d. 1481). Having already seized most of the Balkans (including modern Bosnia and Herzegovina), the Ottoman Turks pushed westward, began a war with Venice (1463–1479), and even briefly occupied the southern Italian city of Otranto. Perhaps as a response to these threatening developments, composers in the West, and particularly those in the orbit of the dukes of Burgundy, began to write large-scale cantus firmus Masses based on a jaunty tune called *L'Homme armé*. The Armed Man tune, and the many Masses built upon it, reflects the militant spirit of the age, when Christians in the West sincerely believed they were about to be overrun by what they viewed as barbarian infidels. But the message of the Armed Man was both broader and more personal than this one militaristic meaning: The Armed Man melody encouraged every good Christian to put on spiritual armor and fight a daily battle against the sins of this world. For this reason, the tune continued to appear as a cantus firmus in polyphonic Masses into the seventeenth century, long after this first, direct threat from the Ottoman Turks had subsided.

Guillaume Dufay's *Missa L'Homme armé* may be the first in the long series of *L'Homme armé* Masses. It is a lengthy and complex work, but one that gains a measure of clarity owing to what becomes an almost rigid use of cantus firmus—the *L'Homme armé* tune—in all five movements of the Mass. On first hearing, the listener may be surprised that the tune, with its call for action and valor, is not more audible. In truth, because the Armed Man tune is in the middle of the texture, which is always difficult to hear, and because it is generally assigned to the lower range of the tenor voice, the tune is not obvious. Only in the "Christe" portion of this *Kyrie*, when we reach the **B** section of the tune and the higher range of the tenor voice, does the melody blare forth like a heroic clarion call. This is a particularly arresting moment, because, while the tune is in triple meter in the "Christe," the metrical context in which it appears is duple. With all this attention paid to the theologically unifying cantus firmus, it is all too easy to fail to recognize that Dufay has surrounded the tune with vocal counterpoint that is both energetic and ingenious. The monophonic tune appears in the "major" mode, although some composers, including Dufay, set it polyphonically in the "minor" mode with B♭.

Guillaume Dufay
a. Tune: *L'Homme armé* (c1460)
CD 2/14

L'homme armé, l'homme armé doibt
   on doubter.
On a fait partout crier,
Que chascun se viegne armer
D'un haubregon de fer.
L'homme armé, l'homme armé doibt
   on doubter.

The armed man, the armed man,
   should be feared.
Everywhere the cry has gone out,
Everyone should arm himself
With a breastplate of iron.
The armed man, the armed man,
   should be feared.

Guillaume Dufay

b. *Kyrie* of the *Missa L'Homme armé* (c1460)

CD 2/15

Chapter 18

Music at the French Royal Court

46

Johannes Ockeghem
Prenez sur moi (c1460)

The galaxy of composers centering around or connected to Johannes Ockeghem—Dufay toward the end of his life, Busnoys, Basiron, Obrecht, and Josquin—was concerned with giving structure to musical works large and small. For the most part, they accomplished this through the imposition of demanding contrapuntal processes such as imitation and canon.

How do you write a three-voice canon such as Ockeghem's *Prenez sur moi*? The leading voice begins, and at some point, in this instance after one measure, the following voice enters, exactly duplicating the leading voice throughout the entire composition, while all the time both voices maintain acceptable counterpoint. When the third voice enters with the theme, keeping the rules of counterpoint becomes even more intricate. The operative term here is "acceptable counterpoint" because the leading and following voices must always conform to the contrapuntal rules that the theorists of the day were just then in the process of writing down in detail. These rules require that consonances occur on strong beats and that dissonance be prepared properly, appearing only quickly and in passing fashion, and then be resolved correctly. By mid-century the consonances are the unison, fifth, octave, third, and sixth. The fourth is thought of as a dissonant interval when occurring between the lowest-sounding pitch and any upper voice. The consistent discipline demonstrated in Ockeghem's *Prenez sur moi* shows how keenly aware composers of the fifteenth century were of these rules. Yet there appear to be a few moments where the composer seems to violate these conventions: he jumps to a dissonance (mm. 21–23, for example) and allows a fourth to sound against the bass on a strong beat (m. 27, for example). Despite these instances where Ockeghem appears a bit lax, this three-voice canon is an impressive accomplishment. If you doubt this is so, try writing an exact canon in fifteenth-century style, incorporating all the rhythmic and melodic idioms of the period!

Johannes Ockeghem
Prenez sur moi (c1460)
CD 2/16

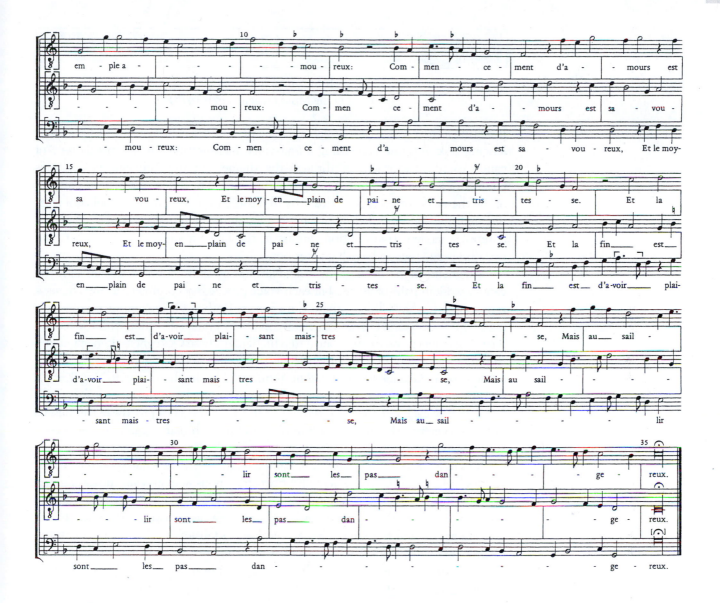

Prenez sur moi vostre exemple amoureux.
Commencement d'amours est savoureux
Et le moyen plain de paine et tristesse,
Et la fin est d'avoir plaisant maistresse,
Mais au saillir sont les pas dangereux.

Take from me your example of love.
The start of love is always tart,
And full of pain and sadness,
And the goal is to have a nice mistress,
But avoid the pitfalls along the way.

Servant Amours, me suis trouvé eureux
L'une des foiz, et l'autre malleureux;
Ung jour sentant confort, l'autre destresse.
Prenez sur moi . . .

Serving Love, I find myself happy
Sometimes faithful, sometimes unhappy;
Feeling comfort one day, distress the next.
Take from me . . .

Pour ung plaisir cent pansers ennuieux,
Pour ung solas cent dangiers perilleux,
Pour ung accueil cent regars par rudesse.
S'Amours sert doncques de telz mets largesse,
Et les loiaux fait les plus douloureux.
Prenez sur moi . . .

For a single pleasure, a hundred tedious thoughts,
For a single comfort, a hundred perilous dangers,
For a single greeting, a hundred rude glances.
Thus Love doles out such desserts in large measure
And the most loyal are made the most unhappy.
Take from me . . .

47

Johannes Ockeghem
Kyrie of the *Missa Prolationum* (c1475)

If writing a three-voice canon such as Ockeghem's *Prenez sur moi* (no. 46) is a challenging task, imagine composing a four-voice mensuration canon. In this type of canon each voice progresses through the theme, but the following voice holds pitches for a longer duration than the leading voice. The different rhythmic patterns of the theme occur because at this time in music history one note symbol could signify multiple durations. Depending upon the original mensuration symbol (time signature), a modern transcription can assign the breve a value that varies between two, three, and four and a half quarter-notes.

Ockeghem's *Kyrie* opens with a double mensuration canon at the unison; the canons work in pairs of voices, but each voice proceeds according to its own mensuration sign. In the "Christe" there is no canon. Rather, Ockeghem first writes two duets, one for alto and bass and then a second for soprano and tenor, with the second duet simply repeating the first one a step higher. To these Ockeghem then appends a third duet for alto and bass, which seems not to be canonic, but in fact does have a free canon embedded in the middle (mm. 58–65). In the return to the "Kyrie," Ockeghem reimposes the process of mensuration canon, but now the interval of imitation within each pair of voices is that of a third. As the Mass progresses through its other movements, the interval of imitation within each pair of canonic voices continues to expand.

More than two centuries later, J.S. Bach used precisely the same procedure in his famous *Goldberg Variations*, where he writes ten canons with an ever-increasing vertical distance between the canonic voices (see *MWC*, Chapter 40). Bach did not know the earlier work by Ockeghem. This is simply a case of two great musical minds arriving at one and the same musical solution. In fairness to the older generation, Ockeghem's contrapuntal achievement is more impressive than Bach's. It requires an almost superhuman mind, or perhaps a computer nowadays, to anticipate the harmonies and avoid the potential dissonances that might occur twenty or thirty measures later as the four voices unfold in pairs of canons, with each voice progressing at its own rate of speed. No wonder the standard musical dictionary in the English language (*The New Grove Dictionary of Music*) calls this work "the most extraordinary contrapuntal achievement of the fifteenth century" (18:318).

Johannes Ockeghem
Kyrie of the Missa Prolationum (c1475)
CD 2/17

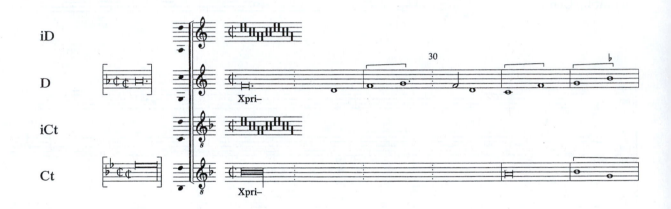

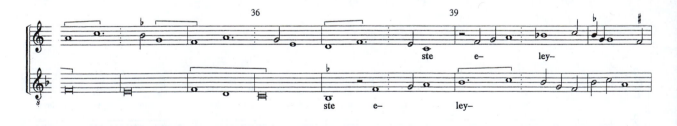

48

Josquin des Prez
Guillaume se va chaufer (c1482)

The music of Josquin des Prez (c1450–1521), one of the towering figures of the Renaissance, will be presented more fully in connection with the Italian city of Ferrara (Chapter 21). But Josquin, as he was known in his day, traveled widely and often. In truth, musicologists are still piecing together—and correcting false assumptions about—Josquin's biography. It is likely that early on in his career, about 1481, Josquin was engaged by Louis XI of France when the king took on the services of a group of singers formerly in the employ of René, duke of Anjou. How long Josquin remained at the French royal court, and how often he returned there, is not entirely certain. Heinrich Glarean, the music theorist who tells the funny tale about the tone-deaf King Louis, probably heard the story and came across Josquin's chanson *Guillaume se va chaufer* (*William is going to warm himself*) when he was a student in Paris in 1517. The piece is as simple as it is amusing. While the tenor voice sings the royal monotone, the bass supports it with a unison D falling to a fifth below (G). Against these two voices, the upper two parts sing a unison canon that is only seven bars long but that repeats three and a half times. According to Glarean, the canon in the upper voices was first sung by two choirboys so as to not overpower the weak voice of the king.

Guillaume se va chaufer   William is going to warm himself
Auprès de la cheminée   close by the chimney
A ung petit de charbon   with a sliver of coal
Qui ne fait point de fumée.   that gives off no smoke at all.

Josquin des Prez
Guillaume se va chaufer (c1482)
CD 2/18

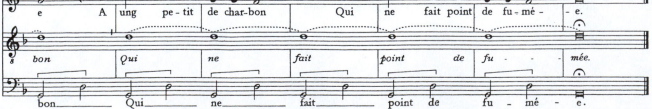

49

Philippe Basiron
Salve, Regina (c1475)

The four-voice *Salve, Regina* by Philippe Basiron (c1449–1491) is a clear example of a paraphrase motet. When writing a musical paraphrase, a composer added a rhythmic profile to the selected melody, usually a preexisting chant, and lightly ornamented the pitches. The paraphrased melody might then be assigned to any voice at any time, and the paraphrase might continue to evolve as the motet proceeded. In his paraphrase of the Marian antiphon *Salve, Regina*, Basiron places the chant (*MWC*, p. 137) in the highest voice, energizing and shaping the plainsong as he proceeds. In measure 9 the alto presents the fourth phrase of the chant (beginning "Ad te suspiramus") in long notes against a repetition of the cantus paraphrase. The tenor enters (m. 10) with a succession of long notes that looks very much like a cantus firmus. If the tenor line is, in fact, a preexisting melody (yet unidentified), it seems not to be drawn from the *Salve, Regina* itself.

Basiron's *Salve, Regina* is actually in two parts; only part one is given here and in the recording. Notice that the recording ends with a slightly different final chord than that given in the score. Two manuscripts preserve this paraphrase motet, one attributing it to Basiron and the other to Ockeghem. These two versions vary slightly in their musical readings. Experts agree, however, that the motet is the work of the younger Basiron, and not of his mentor, Ockeghem.

Philippe Basiron
Salve, Regina (c1475)
CD 2/19

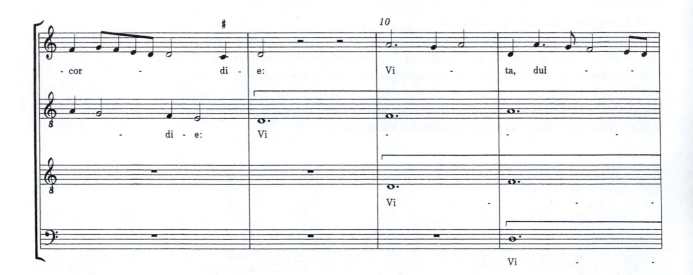

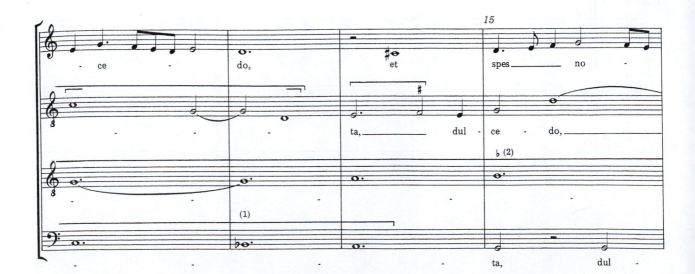

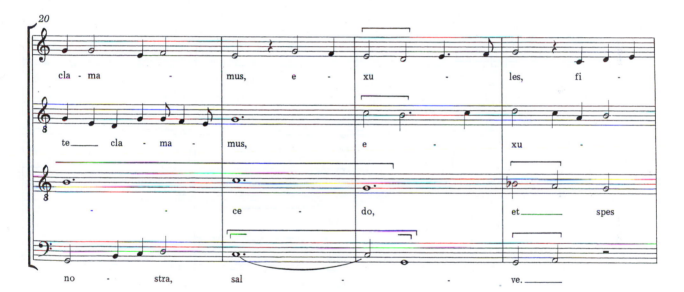

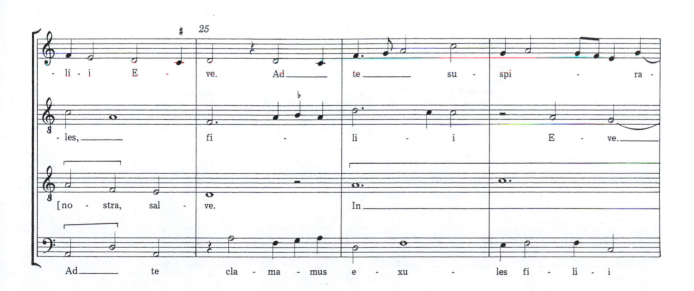

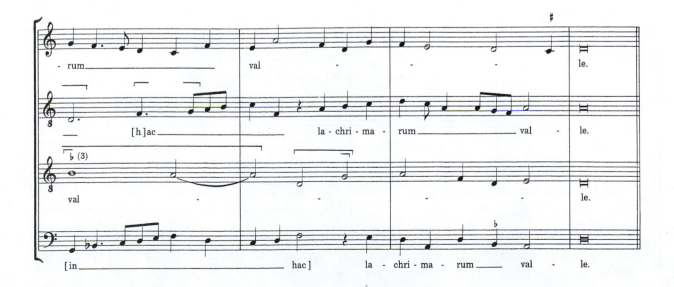

Salve, Regina [Mater] misericordae:	Hail, Queen and mother of mercy,
Vita, dulcedo, et spes nostra, salve.	Hail, our life, comfort, and hope.
Ad te clamamus, exsules, filii Hevae.	Exiled sons of Eve, with loud voice we call upon you.
Ad te suspiramus, gementes et flentes in hac lachrimarum valle.	As we journey in sorrow and lament through this "Valley of Tears," we sigh and long for your help.

Translation from *The Hours of the Divine Office in English and Latin*, vol. 3 (Collegeville, MN: The Liturgical Press, 1963–1965), 112.

50

Antoine Busnoys
Je ne puis vivre ainsy tousjours (c1460)

The introduction of imitation as a compositional technique during the early Renaissance is a development of great importance for the history of music. Imitation had appeared sporadically in the works of Dufay and earlier composers, but not until the generation of Ockeghem and his students did it become commonplace. The very nature of the imitative process—one voice doing more or less what another had done previously—tends to make the voices within a composition more or less equal. Consequently, the older medieval stratification of voices—between a rapidly moving cantus and a slow moving tenor, for example—began to dissolve. With the newer method of imitation, more rapid interchanges might occur among the voices. Such equality of voices and close interaction is clearly evident in Antoine Busnoys' three-voice chanson *Je ne puis vivre ainsy tousjours* (*I cannot live like this forever*). All three voices present the opening theme in imitation. Thereafter, the imitation is mostly confined to the cantus and the tenor. A particularly felicitous moment occurs in bars 25–26 at the very end of the **A** section (and of the piece), where the cantus and tenor ascend a diatonic C scale in imitation, while the contratenor runs down this scale against them. Such stepwise motion is a compositional hallmark of Antoine Busnoys.

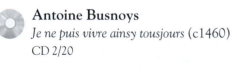

Antoine Busnoys
Je ne puis vivre ainsy tousjours (c1460)
CD 2/20

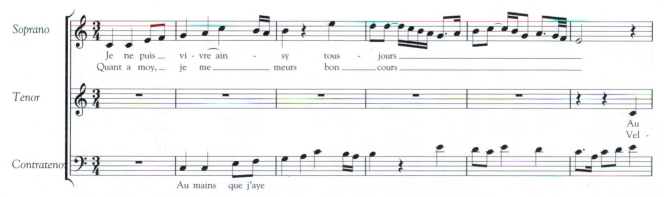

Je ne puis vivre ainsy tousjours	A	I cannot live like this forever
Au mains que j'aye en mes dolours		Unless I have in my distress
Quelque confort,		Some comfort,
Une seulle heure ou mains ou fort;		A single hour, more or less
Et tous les jours		And every day
Léaument serviray Amours		Loyally I will serve Love
Jusqu'a la mort.		Until death.
Noble femme de nom et d'armes	b	Noble woman of name and arms
Escript vous ay ce dittier-cy,		I have written you this ditty
Des jeulx pleurant à chaudes larmes	b	With crying eyes full of warm tears
Affin qu'aiez de moi mercy.		That you may have mercy on me.
Quant a moy, je me meurs bon cours	a	As to me, I waste away apace
Vellant les nuytz, faisant cent tours,		Awake at nights, tossing a hundred times,
En criant fort:		And crying loudly:
"Vengeance!" a Dieu, car a grant tort		Vengeance! by God, because wrongly
Je noye en plours		I drown in tears
Lorsqu'au besoing me fault secours,		While in need I lack succor
Et Pitié dort.		And Pity sleeps.
Je ne puis vivre ainsy tousjours . . .	A	I cannot live like this forever . . .

Music in the Low Countries

51

Jacob Obrecht
Credo of the Missa Sub tuum presidium (c1500)

Jacob Obrecht's *Missa Sub tuum presidium* reveals yet another face of the "constructivist" persona of northern composers during the late fifteenth century—the capacity to superimpose several preexisting melodies and thereby create a Mass or motet with more than one cantus firmus. If one cantus firmus might serve as a signifier of theological intent with a religious composition, why not place several at once to convey various complementary religious themes? As is true of most polyphonic Masses from the late Middle Ages and Renaissance, Obrecht's *Missa Sub tuum presidum* provides a polyphonic setting for the five movements of the Ordinary of the Mass: *Kyrie, Gloria, Credo, Sanctus,* and *Agnus dei.*

It begins with a *Kyrie* for three voices (perhaps signifying the Trinity) and ends with an *Agnus dei* for seven (the symbolic number of the Virgin at that time). As more and more voices are added, so, too, are more and more cantus firmi, until four appear together in the concluding *Agnus dei.* For the *Credo,* Obrecht employs five vocal parts, and places a separate cantus firmus in each of the upper two parts. Singing the Latin chant *Audi nos* (*Hear us*), Cantus 2 implores Jesus for mercy, while Cantus 1 invokes the chant *Sub tuum presidium* (*Under Your Protection*) that asks the Virgin to intercede before her son on behalf of all sinners. The chant *Sub tuum presidium* is the principal cantus firmus of Obrecht's Mass; it appears in the top voice in all five movements.

The image that it calls forth is that of Our Lady of the Protecting Cloak, under whose mantle all humanity may gather. This religious theme would be transformed into an icon of the Catholic Church, depicted by Renaissance artists in countless paintings, statues, and altarpieces, particularly in Italy, Spain, and the New World.

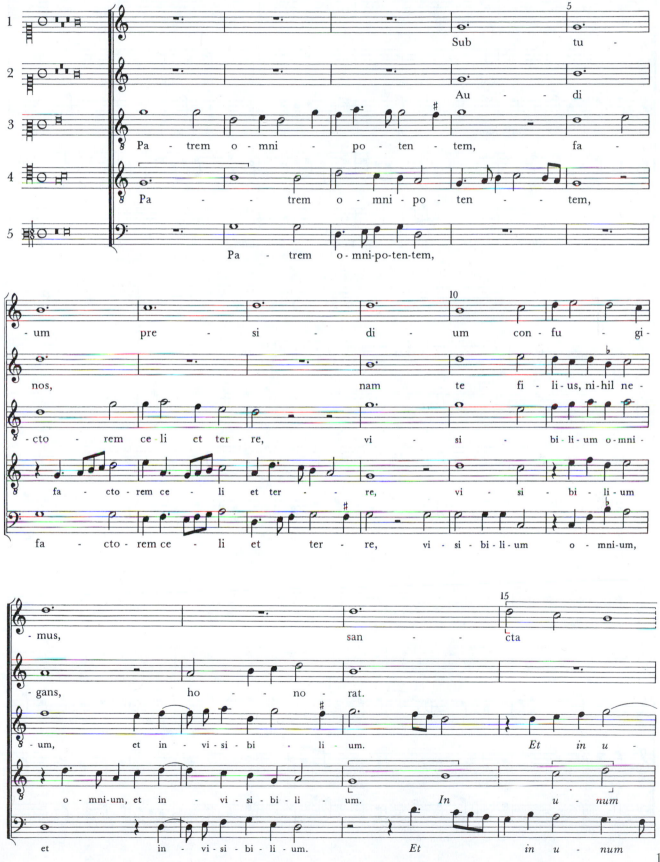

[Credo in unum Deum,] Patrem omnipotentem,	[I believe in one God,] the Father Almighty,
factorem caeli et terrae,	Maker of heaven and earth,
visibilium omnium et invisibilium.	And of all things visible and invisible:
Et in unum Dominum Jesum Christum Filium Dei unigenitum.	And in one Lord Jesus Christ, the only-begotten Son of God;
Et ex Patre natum ante omnia saecula,	Begotten of his Father before all worlds,
Deum de Deo, lumen de lumine, Deum verum de Deo vero,	God of God, Light of Light, very God of very God,
[Genitum, non factum, consubstantialem Patri:	[Begotten, not made, being of one substance with the Father;
per quem omnia facta sunt.	By whom all things were made:
Qui propter nos homines et propter nostram salutem descendit de caelis,	Who for us men and for our salvation came down from heaven.
Et incarnatus est de Spiritu Sancto ex Maria Virgine: et homo factus est.	And was incarnate by the Holy Ghost of the Virgin Mary, and was made man:
Crucifixus etiam pro nobis: sub Pontio Pilato passus, et sepultus est.]	And was crucified also for us under Pontius Pilate; He suffered and was buried:]
Et resurrexit tertia die, secundum Scripturas.	And the third day he rose again according to the Scriptures:
Et ascendit in caelum:	And ascended into heaven,
sedet ad dexteram Patris.	And sitteth on the right hand of the Father:
Et iterum venturus est cum gloria	And he shall come again, with glory,
judicare vivos et mortuos:	to judge both the quick and the dead;
cujus regni non erit finis.	Whose kingdom shall have no end.
[Et in Spiritum Sanctum, Dominum, et vivificantem:	[And [I believe] in the Holy Ghost, the Lord, and Giver of life,
qui ex Patre, Filioque procedit.	Who proceedeth from the Father and the Son;
Qui cum Patre, et Filio simul adoratur, et conglorificatur:	Who with the Father and the Son together is worshiped and glorified;
qui locutus est per Prophetas.	Who spake by the Prophets:
Et unam sanctam catholicam et apostolicam Ecclesiam.	And [I believe] one holy Catholic and Apostolic Church:
Confiteor unum baptisma	I acknowledge one Baptism
in remissionem peccatorum.	for the remission of sins:
Et exspecto resurrectionem mortuorum.]	And I look for the resurrection of the dead:]
Et vitam venturi saeculi. Amen.	And the life of the world to come. Amen.

Chant

Sub tuum presidium configimus,
sancta Dei Genitrix:
nostras deprecationes ne despicias in
   necessitatibus.
Sed a periculis libera nos semper,
   Virgo benedicta.

Under your protection we gather,
holy progenitor of God:
be mindful of our prayers during this time
   of need.
But from all dangers always free us,
   blessed Virgin.

Chant

Audi nos, nam te filius, nihil negans,
   honorat.
Salva nos, Iesu, pro quibus virgo mater te
   orat.

Hear us, for the all-giving Son,
   honors you.
Save us, Jesus, we for whom the Virgin
   Mother prays.

52

Heinrich Isaac
La Spagna (c1500)

La Spagna was one of the "hit tunes" of the late fifteenth century. Among the numerous composers who provided it with a polyphonic setting was Heinrich Isaac (c1450–1517), whom we shall meet again in Chapter 24. As is appropriate for a *basse danse*, Isaac places the tune in the lowest part, where it could easily be played by a sackbut. Like a tenor cantus firmus, the melody sounds forth in equal notes of long duration, and during each of these the dancers would have executed one or another of the standard dance steps of the *basse danse* (see MWC, p. 144). Above the tune, Isaac added two lively voices that banter back and forth in quick imitation. On this recording the middle part is played on a shawm and the top part on a cornett. (About these instruments, see MWC, Chapter 23). Notice that on this recording, once the performers have played through Isaac's arrangement, they repeat it, and as they repeat, they begin to add ornaments to the written score. Supplemental ornamentation was a convention of Renaissance instrumental music, as was the addition of percussion.

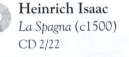

Heinrich Isaac
La Spagna (c1500)
CD 2/22

5

9

13

17

THE LATE RENAISSANCE

Chapter
20

Popular Music in Florence, 1470–1540
Carnival Song and Lauda, Frottola, and Early Madrigal

53

Lorenzo de' Medici (text)
Sian galanti di Valenza (c1490)

Music in Western Civilization discusses mostly what might be called "learned" or "high art" music—the type of music that requires extensive compositional training and considerable forethought to create. The first three pieces in Chapter 20 offer a different legacy of human musical creativity and compositional processing. They contain a vestige of improvisatory practices and suggest a more popular, less learned origin. One sure sign of the popular influence in Florentine Renaissance music is the use of homophonic texture made up of simple chords—chords that might result from a straightforward strumming on an accompanying string instrument. Note that in *Sian galanti di Valenza*, a carnival song with text by Lorenzo de' Medici, almost all of the chords are what we today would call triads in root position. This suggests spontaneous improvisation, perhaps one occurring on the streets of Florence. Only later did the process, now turned into "the composition," get tidied up and written down in a music manuscript. By odd coincidence, another type of unwritten popular music— that of early rhythm and blues and the doo-wop sound coming out of Detroit and New York during the 1950s—is also comprised exclusively of triads in root position.

Lorenzo de' Medici (text)
Sian galanti di Valenza (c1490)
CD 3/1

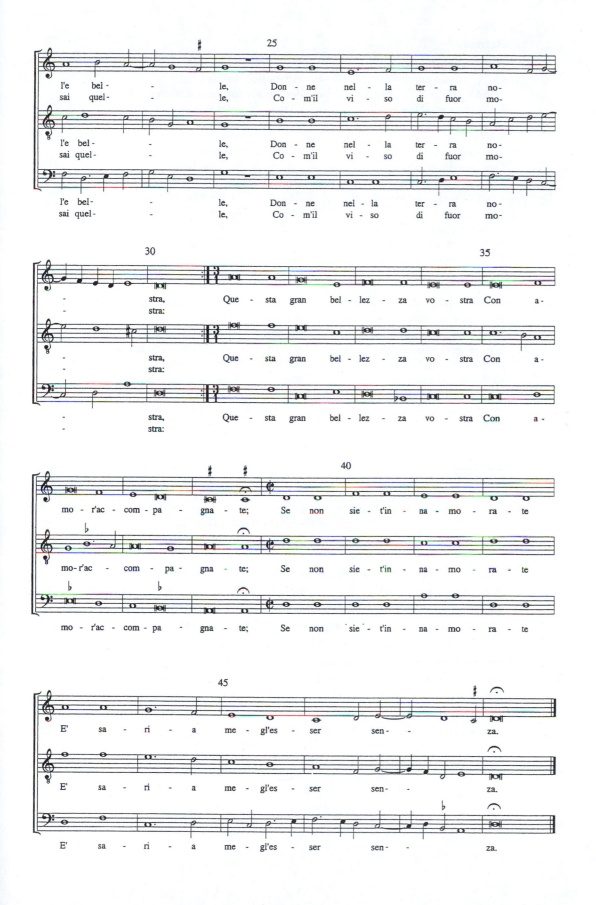

Refrain

Sian galanti di Valenza,	a	We are the gallants of Valencia,
Qui per passo capitati,	b	Just passing through,
D'amor già presi e legati	b	But already caught and bound in the love
Delle donne di Fiorenza.	a	Of the women of Florence.

Stanza 1

Son molto gentil'e belle,	Most noble and beautiful
Donne nella terra nostra,	Are the ladies in our land,
Voi vincete d'assai quelle,	But you surpass them by far,
Com'il viso di fuor mostra:	As can be seen from your face,
Questa gran bellezza vostra	Your great beauty
Con amor' accompagnate;	Accompanied by love;
Se non siet' innamorate	It would be better
E' saria megl' esser senza.	To be without.

Stanza 2

Donne, ciò che abbiamo è vostro,	Ladies, all we have is yours;
Se d'amor voi siate accese,	If you are fired by love,
Metterem l'olio di nostro,	We will give you the oil ourselves.
Ungeremo a nostre spese.	We will give you the ointment at our expense.
Abbiam olio del paese,	We have oils from our land,
Gelsi, aranci e bengiuì:	Mulberry, orange, and benzoin perfume:
Se vi piace, proviam qui:	If they please you, give them a try here;
Fate questa esperienza.	Take advantage of this experience.

54

Girolamo Savonarola (text)
Giesù, sommo conforto (c1495)

The lauda *Giesù, sommo conforto*, setting a text by Girolamo Savonarola, is like the preceding carnival song—a clear example of Florentine popular music. In fact, this lauda presents an even more rudimentary type of harmony, for here each and every chord is in what we would call a root position. *Giesù, sommo conforto* began as a carnival song, and sometime around 1495 the original secular lyrics were replaced by the sacred words of Savonarola. At first there was most likely just the tune; to this someone improvised a lower support and another person a counterpoint at the interval of a third or a fourth. On our recording, this lauda is presented in just that fashion. First the tune is sung, then it appears with tenor support, and finally with an alto line weaving both above and below it.

Girolamo Savonarola (text)
Giesù, sommo conforto (c1495)
CD 3/2

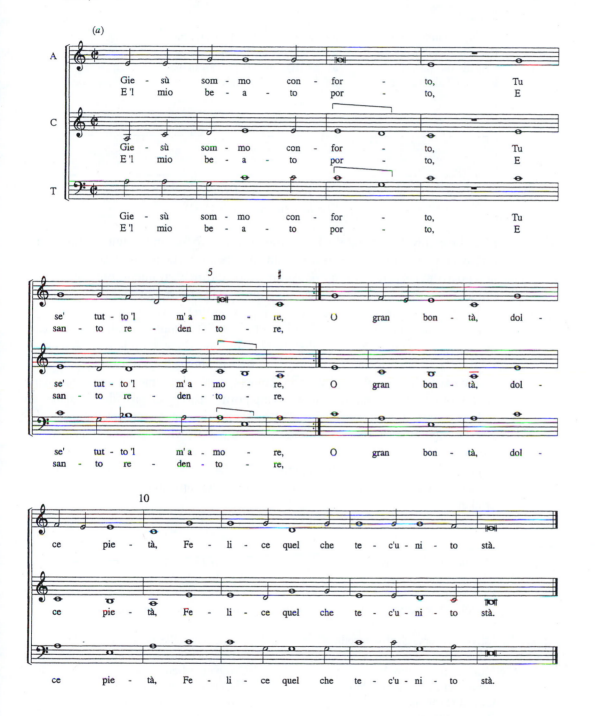

Verse 1

Giesù, sommo conforto,	a	Jesu, highest solace,
Tu se' tutto'l m' amore	b	You are all my love,
E 'l mio beato porto	a	And my blessed refuge
E santo redentore.	b	And holy redeemer.

Refrain

O gran bontà, dolce pietà	c	O great goodness, sweet mercy,
Felice quel che tec' unito stà!	c	Happy the one united with you!

Verse 2

O Croce, fammi loco	a	O Cross, make a place for me
E le mie membra prendi,	d	And take my limbs,
Che del tuo santo foco	a	So that my heart and soul may
E 'l cor e l'alma accendi.	d	Burn with your holy fire.

55

Josquin des Prez
El grillo è bon cantore (c1500)

Like the carnival song and the lauda, the frottola is rooted in the improvisatory traditions of Italian music. The frottola came into being as the result of singing vernacular poetry *ex tempore* to the accompaniment of a string instrument. But the frottola, unlike the carnival song and lauda, was improvised at court, not in the streets.

The frottola *El grillo* (*The Cricket*) by Josquin des Prez reveals its improvisatory origins in the use of root position chords exclusively. This could be dull music indeed, but Josquin ingeniously saves the day by infusing these chords with infectious rhythms and zesty textual repetition (what we will later call "patter-song").

Typically, the frottola is a strophic composition—the same music serves many stanzas of text. However, the sole surviving print of this piece provides *El grillo* with only one verse of text and a refrain. The music involves many repeats, but musicologists have pointed out that it is difficult to know exactly what should be repeated and when.

As to the meaning of the text, perhaps it alludes to sexual activity in the heat of summer, perhaps to papal singer Carlo Grillo, or perhaps it's just a fun song about a cricket.

El grillo è bon cantore	The cricket is a good singer
Che tiene longo verso.	Who has a long cry.
Dale beve grillo canta.	The cricket sings of drinking.
El grillo è bon cantore.	The cricket is a good singer.
Ma non fa come gli altri uccelli,	But he is not, like other birds,
Come li han cantato un poco,	When they have sung a little,
Van' de fatto in altro loco.	Go off elsewhere.
Sempre el grillo sta pur saldo.	The cricket stays still.
Quando la maggior el caldo	When the weather is hotter
Alhor canta sol per amore.	Then he sings for love.
El grillo è bon cantore	The cricket is a good singer
Che tiene longo verso.	Who has a long cry.
Dale beve grillo canta.	The cricket sings of drinking.
El grillo è bon cantore.	The cricket is a good singer.

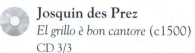

Josquin des Prez
El grillo è bon cantore (c1500)
CD 3/3

56

Jacques Arcadelt
Il bianco e dolce cigno (c1538)

The madrigal was the most popular form of learned vocal music in Italy during the sixteenth century, when literally thousands of madrigals were printed. Most characteristic of the madrigal is the close bond between text and music. While Josquin des Prez begins to include this sort of text expression in his motets (no. 59), the madrigalists indulged in an abundance of overt onomatopoetic expression—the music tries to sound out nearly every word of the text. Thus, when the madrigal text says "chase after" or "follow quickly," the music becomes fast and one voice chases after another in musical imitation. For such words as "pain," "anguish," "death," and "cruel fate," the madrigal composer invariably will employ a biting dissonance or a twisting chromatic scale. These are the musical brushstrokes involved in word painting through music.

What drove composers to develop this newfound expressivity? While there was no single cause, one important reason lay in the cultural climate of the 1520s and 1530s. Throughout the fifteenth century, Latin had been the preferred language of the Italian humanists; however, during the first decades of the sixteenth century, the humanists turned their attention to vernacular texts, and sought literary models in the great Tuscan Italian writers of the fourteenth century, especially Petrarch (for poetry) and Boccaccio (for prose). Composers wished to match serious poetry with serious music, and indeed the sixteenth-century madrigal generally develops a more serious tone than the other types of secular vocal music written at this time, such as the frottola.

Jacques Arcadelt's *Il bianco e dolce cigno* (*The gentle white swan*) was among the first madrigals published, and thus its onomatopoetic gestures are modest. A striking chord on the word "piangendo" ("weeping"; mm. 6 and 11), a 7–6 suspension on "sento" ("I feel"; m. 33), and a satisfying plagal (Amen) cadence for the concluding "contento" ("contented"; mm. 45–46) are the principal moments of word painting. This is high-quality poetry treated with musical sensitivity, and it created something of a sensation. *Il bianco e dolce cigno* was reprinted more than fifty times, and several later composers used it as a point of departure for new settings of the same text.

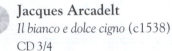

Jacques Arcadelt
Il bianco e dolce cigno (c1538)
CD 3/4

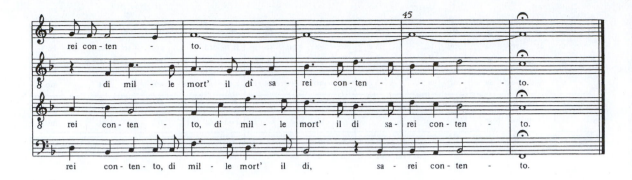

Il bianco e dolce cigno	The gentle white swan
Cantando more, et io	dies singing, and I,
Piangendo giung' al fin del viver mio,	weeping, approach the end of my life.
Stran' e diversa sorte!	Strange and diverse fates,
Ch'ei more sconsolato,	that he dies disconsolate,
Et io moro beato,	and I die happy.
Morte che nel morire	Death, that in the [act of] dying
M'empie di gioia tutt'e di desire.	fills me wholly with joy and desire.
Se nel morir, altro dolor non sento,	If in dying I feel no other pain,
Di mille mort' il di, sarei contento.	I would be content to die a thousand deaths a day.

57

Orazio Vecchi
Il bianco e dolce cigno (1589)

The continuing influence of Arcadelt's *Il bianco e dolce cigno* (no. 56) can be seen in Orazio Vecchi's setting of the same text. Vecchi received a musical education from the monks of the Italian city of Modena, and himself became a priest. But among his contemporaries, Vecchi achieved a reputation not with religious music, but through his numerous settings of secular poems that he shaped into madrigals and into two lighter musical genres called the canzonetta and villanella. Vecchi's setting of *Il bianco e dolce cigno* demonstrates the extremes to which some Italian madrigalists might go when indulging in word painting. Instead of respecting the overall tenor of the poem, as had Arcadelt, Vecchi dismembers individual words and phrases, subjecting each to an "over the top" treatment. His catalogue of madrigalisms includes a lyrical melisma on "cantando" ("singing"; m. 6), the expected bold shift on "piangendo" ("weeping"; m. 20), a triple-meter dance on "beato" ("blessed"; mm. 41–45), another joyful melisma on "gioia" ("joy"; m. 52), and so on. The result is an exaggerated, disjointed work that borders on the comical. Perhaps Vecchi intended his madrigal as homage to Arcadelt. Perhaps he meant it to be a parody—one work of art poking fun at another. You decide.

Orazio Vecchi
Il bianco e dolce cigno (1589)
CD 3/5

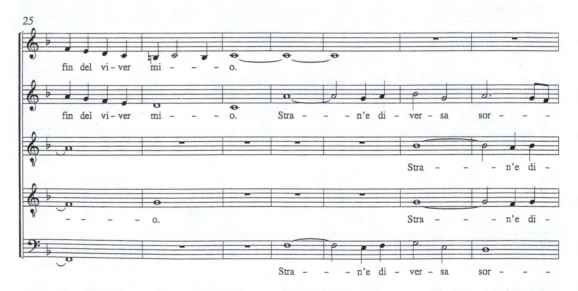

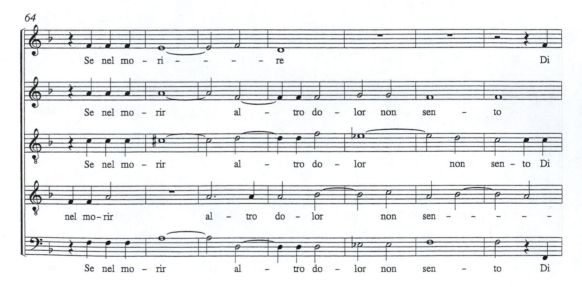

Il bianco e dolce cigno
Cantando more, ed io
Piangendo giong' al fin del viver mio,
Stran'e diversa sorte!
Ch'ei more sconsolato,
Ed io moro beato,
Morte che nel morire
M'empie di gioia tutt'e di desire.
Se nel morir', altro dolor non sento,
Di mille mort'il di, sarei contento.

The gentle white swan
dies singing, and I,
weeping, approach the end of my life.
Strange and diverse fates,
that he dies disconsolate,
and I die happy.
Death, that in the [act of] dying
fills me wholly with joy and desire.
If in dying I feel no other pain,
I would be content to die a thousand
    deaths a day.

Chapter 21

Josquin des Prez and Music in Ferrara

58

Josquin des Prez
Sanctus of the *Missa Hercules dux Ferrarie* (c1503?)

The method by which Josquin des Prez carved out his *soggetto cavato dalle vocali* ("subject cut out from the vowels") is discussed in detail in MWC (p. 160). In brief, Josquin extracted the vowels in the name of his patron and, equating them with the notes of the Guidonian hexachord, created a musical theme. At the beginning of the *Sanctus,* the composer places the ducal theme first in the alto in long notes, and then in the tenor. For the succeeding section, "Pleni sunt coeli," he creates a straightforward canon between the alto and bass that alludes to the theme, but does not quote it directly. Notice in this section a technique frequently found in the works of Josquin: Near the end of a passage of text, the note values get smaller and melodic sequences push the music higher and higher, resulting in a splendid drive toward the final cadence. Similarly, in the section "Hosanna in excelsis" the theme (now in the tenor) appears in long notes at the beginning but in halved values at the end. Again, the effect is a rhythmic acceleration toward the final cadence.

In the impressive "Hosanna," the theme is positioned to begin on d, a, and d' thus creating a twenty-four-note chain, d-c-d-c-d-f-e-d, a-g-a-g-a-c'-b-a, d'-c'-d'-c'-d'-f'-e'-d', as the duke's name is musically reiterated. Here, as is often the case in music, rising melodic sequence and rhythmic diminution create a sense of growing excitement. Following the brief two-voice "Benedictus," the grand four-voice "Hosanna" is repeated. This repetition is not included in the recording, but to hear the passage again, simply return to that part of the track. Every *Sanctus* must end with a triumphant "Hosanna in excelsis" ("Glory be to God in the highest").

Josquin des Prez
Sanctus of the *Missa Hercules dux Ferrarie* (c1503?)
CD 3/6

201

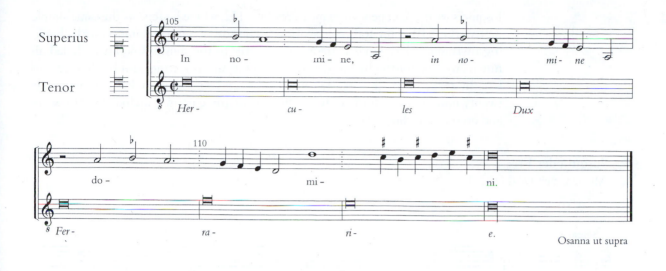

Osanna ut supra

Sanctus, sanctus, sanctus,	Holy, holy, holy,
Dominus Deus Sabaoth.	Lord God almighty.
Pleni sunt coeli et terra gloria tua	The heavens and earth are filled with your glory
Hosanna in excelsis.	Hosanna in the highest.
Benedictus qui venit in nomine domini.	Blessed is he who comes in the name of the Lord.
Hosanna in excelsis.	Hosanna in the highest.

59

Josquin des Prez
Miserere mei, Deus (1503)
(Prima pars)

Although Josquin des Prez composed in all of the musical genres of his day, his most remarkable compositions are perhaps his seventy-odd surviving motets. In these, Josquin composes in a manner that is text expressive, that is to say a method in which he uses music to intensify the meaning of a vivid phrase of text or a poetic image. This is quite different from the abstract and sometimes number-based symbolism of the late Middle Ages, and it points toward the text-expressive word painting that will be cultivated by madrigal composers in the later Renaissance.

The text of *Miserere mei, Deus* is, of course, not Josquin's own but rather comes from Psalm 50 (Protestant Psalm 51) as found in the Old Testament. Verses such as "Thou shalt sprinkle me with hyssop [O Lord], and I shall be cleansed: Thou shalt wash me, and I shall be made whiter than snow" provide vivid imagery, especially when surrounded by the mournful refrain "Miserere mei, Deus" ("Have mercy on me, O God"). The sorrowful tone of the motet is established at the outset by the use of a half-step inflection, a traditional sign of lamentation. Other instances of text painting include the isolation of the word "dele" ("take away"; m. 35), the fullness of sound on "amplius lava me" ("wash me fully"; m. 46); and the reduction of the texture to just two voices for "tibi soli" ("you alone", bar 79). A particular hallmark of

Josquin's writing can be seen in measures 115–132, where he repeats the same simple motive (G,A,B) in the top voice six times. This sort of musical iteration with changing rhythmic values lends extraordinary power to the music. Josquin included all nineteen verses of the psalm *Miserere mei, Deus* in his setting, and he divided this lengthy text into three parts. Because the entire composition takes approximately twenty minutes to perform, only the first of the three parts is included in the score and on the recording.

Josquin des Prez
Miserere mei, Deus (1503)
CD 3/7

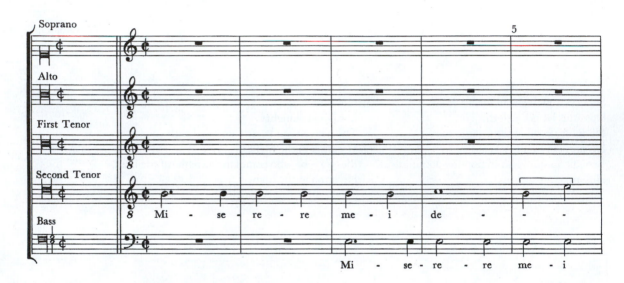

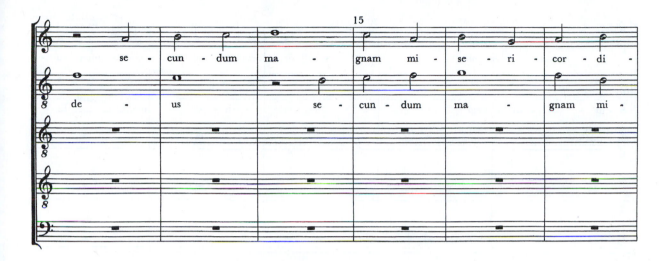

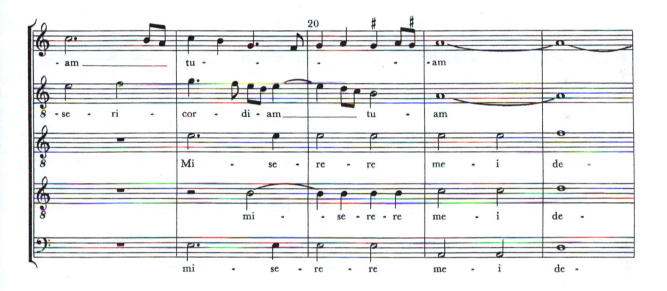

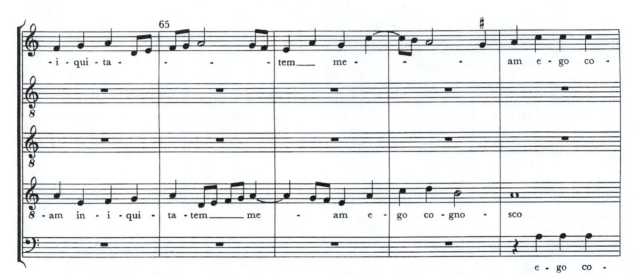

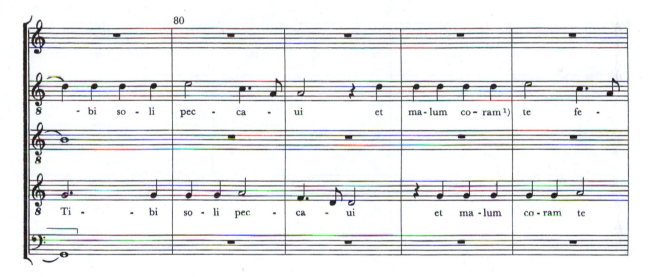

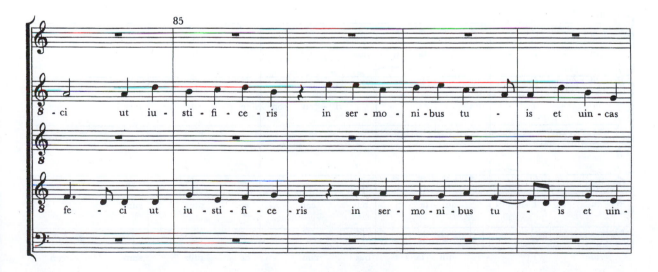

[1] Orig.: coran.

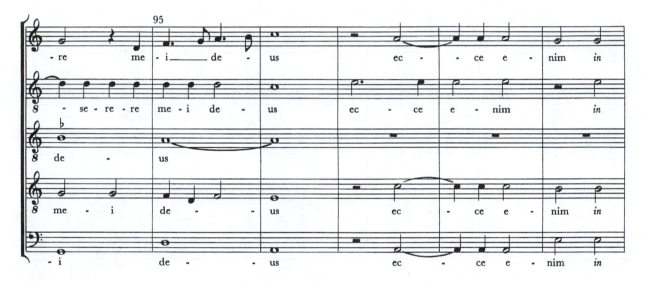

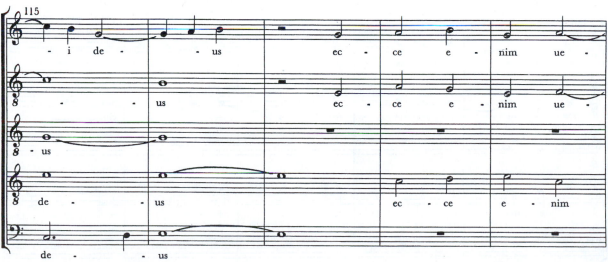

2 The manuscript repeats here the words "et in peccatis."

120
- ri - ta - tem di - le - xi - Sti in - cer - ta
- ri - ta - tem di - le - xsi Sti in - cer - ta
ue - ri - ta - tem di - le - Xi - sti in - cer -

125
et o - cul - ta sa - pi - en - ti - e tu - e
et o - cul - ta sa - pi - en - ti - e tu - e
- ta et o - cul - ta sa - pi - en - ti - e tu -

130
ma - ni - fe - sta - sti mi - -
ma - ni - fe - sta - sti mi - chi
- e ma - ni - fe - sta - sti mi -

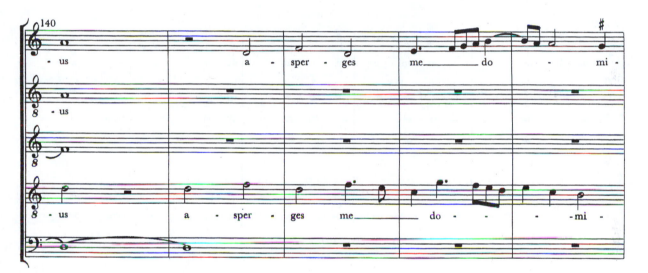

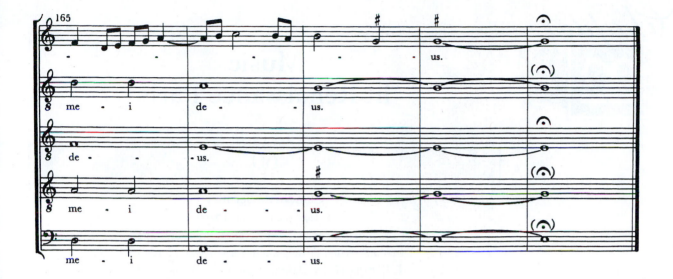

Miserere mei, Deus, secundum magnam miserecordiam tuam.	Have mercy on me, O God, according to Thy great mercy.
Miserere mei, Deus.	Have mercy on me, O God.
Et secundum multitudinem miserationum tuarum dele iniquitatem meam.	And according to the multitude of Thy tender mercies, blot out my iniquity.
Miserere mei, Deus.	Have mercy on me, O God.
Amplius lava me ab iniquitate mea et a peccato meo munda me.	Wash me yet more from my iniquity, and cleanse me from my sin.
Miserere mei, Deus.	Have mercy on me, O God.
Quoniam iniquitatem meam ego cognosco, et peccatum meum contra me est semper.	For I know my iniquity, and my sin is always before me.
Miserere mei, Deus.	Have mercy on me, O God.
Tibi soli peccavi et malum coram te feci, ut iustificeris in sermonibus tuis et vincas cum iudicaris.	To Thee only have I sinned, and have done evil before Thee: that Thou mayst be justified in Thy words, and mayst overcome when Thou are judged.

Miserere mei, Deus, secundum magnam
  miserecordiam tuam.
Miserere mei, Deus.
Et secundum multitudinem miserationum
  tuarum dele iniquitatem meam.
Miserere mei, Deus.
Amplius lava me ab iniquitate mea et a
  peccato meo munda me.
Miserere mei, Deus.
Quoniam iniquitatem meam ego cognosco,
  et peccatum meum contra me est semper.
Miserere mei, Deus.
Tibi soli peccavi et malum coram te feci, ut
  iustificeris in sermonibus tuis et vincas
  cum iudicaris.

Miserere mei, Deus.
Ecce enim iniquitatibus conceptus sum,
  et in peccatis concepit me mater mea.
Miserere mei, Deus.
Ecce enim veritatem dilexisti,
  incerta et occulta sapientiae tuae
  manifestasti mihi.
Miserere mei, Deus.
Asperges me, Domine, hyssopo, et
  mundabor; lavabis me, et super nivem
  dealbabor.

Miserere mei, Deus.

Have mercy on me, O God, according to
  Thy great mercy.
Have mercy on me, O God.
And according to the multitude of Thy
  tender mercies, blot out my iniquity.
Have mercy on me, O God.
Wash me yet more from my iniquity,
  and cleanse me from my sin.
Have mercy on me, O God.
For I know my iniquity, and my sin is always
  before me.
Have mercy on me, O God.
To Thee only have I sinned, and have done
  evil before Thee: that Thou mayst be
  justified in Thy words, and mayst
  overcome when Thou are judged.
Have mercy on me, O God.
For behold I was conceived in iniquities:
  and in sin did my mother conceive me.
Have mercy on me, O God.
For behold Thou hast loved truth: the
  uncertain and hidden things of Thy
  wisdom Thou hast made manifest to me.
Have mercy on me, O God.
Thou shalt sprinkle me with hyssop
  [O Lord], and I shall be cleansed: Thou
  shalt wash me, and I shall be made whiter
  than snow.
Have mercy on me, O God.

Chapter 22

Music in Renaissance Paris

60

Claudin de Sermisy
a. *Tant que vivray* (c1528)
b. *Tant que vivray:* Arrangement for lute (1529)
c. *Tant que vivray:* Arrangement for voice and lute (1529)
d. *Tant que vivray:* Arrangement for keyboard (1531)

Claudin de Sermisy's four-voice song *Tant que vivray* (*As Long as I Live*) is a fine representative of a genre of music called the Parisian chanson. The sixteenth-century Parisian chanson was social music intended to be performed by educated musicians—those who could read music—in a variety of social settings ranging from the court to the merchant's home to the student's lodgings. If women generally were barred from singing Masses and motets in churches at this time, there was no such ban with regard to the Parisian chanson. This was music for both upper- and middle-class environments and for performers of both sexes, as Figure 22-2 (MWC, p. 169) suggests.

Claudin de Sermisy, though a priest, wrote secular songs that became wildly popular, among them his beautiful *Tant que vivray*. But there is an element of ambiguity here. Where is the melody? Is it in the alluring tenor line, or in the equally charming cantus? The traditional struggle for melodic primacy between the tenor and soprano was still being played out during the sixteenth century. In some popular songs of the early 1500s, the tune is in the tenor (see no. 64a, for example); in others it is in the cantus. Yet there is an air of familiarity here as well. Harmonic progressions that we would today identify as IV–V–I appear frequently at cadences. Indeed, it is in the popular songs of the sixteenth century that what we today call functional harmonic progressions can be seen in their most rudimentary form for the first time.

It is axiomatic in music history that once a song becomes popular, instrumental arrangements of it will appear. Thus, the publisher of *Tant que vivray* (1528), Pierre Attaingnant, soon produced versions of his best-seller intended for lute (1529), for lute and voice (1529), and for keyboard instrument (1531). In general, these intabulations tend to fill with instrumental ornamentation moments of sound originally sustained by the voices. It is likely that during the Renaissance, musicians would have added even more embellishments, especially if the song was repeated.

Claudin de Sermisy
a. *Tant que vivray* (c1528)
CD 3/8

Tant que vivray en aage florissant,	So long as I'm in the prime of life,
Je serviray d'amours le roy puissant	I will serve the powerful king of love
En faictz, en ditz, en chansons et accordz.	In art and poetry, and in song and harmony.
Par plusiers jours m'a tenu languissant,	Several times in the past I've been blue,
Et puis après duel ma fait resjoyssant,	But, melancholy passed, I rejoiced again,
Car j'ay l'amour de la belle au gent corps.	For I have the love of a beautiful noble lady.
Son alliance,	Her allegiance,
C'est ma fiance.	That is my faith.
Son coeur est mien,	Her heart is mine,
Le mien est sien,	And mine is hers.
Fy de tristesse,	Dispatch all care,
Vive liesse,	May joy live long,
Puisqu'en amours a tant de biens.	Since there is much good in love.

Claudin de Sermisy
b. *Tant que vivray:* Arrangement for lute (1529)
Thomson-Schirmer Website

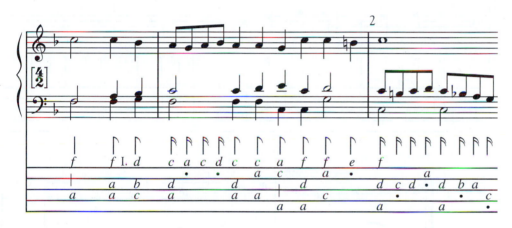

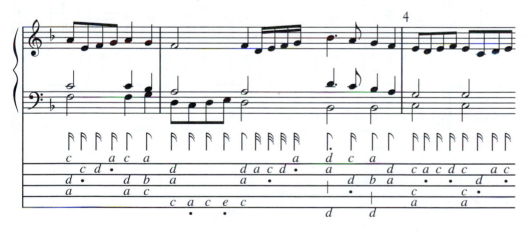

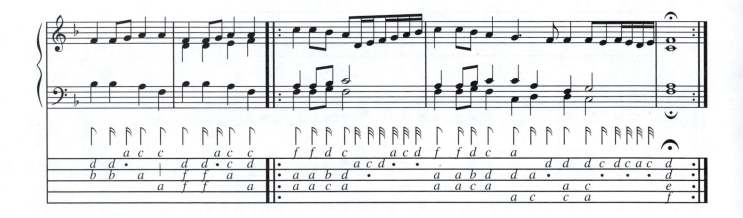

Claudin de Sermisy

c. Tant que vivray: Arrangement for voice and lute (1529)

CD 3/9

[T]ant   que   vi . vray   en   aa . ge   flo . ris .
Par   plu . sieurs   iours   m'a   te . nu   lan . guis .

. sant   Ie   ser . vi . ray   d'a .
. sant   Mais   a . pres   dueil   m'a

(1)

. mour   le   dieu   puis . sant   En   faitz, en   dictz_____ en   chan .
faict   re . iou . is . sant   Car   i'ay   l'a . mour   de   la   bel .

(2)

(1) The e' is a quarter note in the tablature.   (2) The original is a c'.

Claudin de Sermisy

d. *Tant que vivray:* Arrangement for keyboard (1531)
Thomson-Schirmer Website

f.58

61

Anonymous
a. Pavane (1547)
b. Galliard (1547)

Thoinot Arbeau's *Orchésographie* was written as a conversation between an old dancing master, who happens to be a priest, and a young man who wishes to learn the art of social dancing. It offers a gold mine of advice, from the types of clothing that were appropriate for different dances to describing the correct manner for a man to ask a woman to dance, and even what was proper to think if he was turned down! However, the heart of the book was given to describing steps to various dances, including the pavane and galliard.

To dance the pavane, the couple faces forward with the man on the left and the woman on his right and moves with their near hands joined together. In its simplest form, the pavane consists of continuous groups of two *simples* (ss) and one *double* (d) for the duration of the dance. It requires four measures of music to complete two *simples* with one step per bar: left, right, right, left. In executing the *simple*, it is important to remember that *the heels never pass each other* as if walking, but always stop together before proceeding to the next pair of steps. The *double* also requires four bars, but the steps are left, right, left, right. After proceeding three paces, the fourth step simply brings the right foot up together with the left. The dance therefore consists of stringing together groups of two *simples* and one *double* (ss d ss d ss d etc.). At the conclusion of an eight-bar section, the couple either reverses direction or, if the hall is too crowded, continues moving forward. (Arbeau recommended always moving forward, because the woman might trip when moving backward, and he warned his male readers that after such a *faux pas,* they would suffer an equally precipitous fall in feminine favor. Chances are he spoke from experience.)

The dance would continue until the couples had circled the hall two or three times. The men, if they were aristocratic, were allowed to wear a cloak and sword, and all could wear their ceremonial garments on special days. Great ladies of the court were allowed to have servants walk behind them carrying their long trains. A large group was not required to dance the pavane, but if a couple danced alone, Arbeau suggested they select a tune that moved at a faster tempo.

The galliard was not only a livelier dance, with plenty of kicks and leaps, it was also more complicated. While Arbeau was able to describe the steps of the pavane on a single page, he required fifteen to explain the galliard. It was a dance that demanded agility, significant powers of endurance, and flamboyant self-confidence—all traits more frequently found among the young than their elders. One move in particular, the capriole, is worthy of comment. This difficult jump could be performed only by dancers with excellent coordination. During the leap that occurred just prior to the cadence, dancers would move their feet about in the air prior to landing. If done well, it could excite admiration; however, a poor execution would appear ungainly and likely result in a fall. Centuries later, this particular piece of choreographic embellishment was mentioned in Mozart's opera *Le nozze di Figaro*. In the aria "Se vuol ballare" (no. 137a), Figaro promises to make the devious Count Almaviva perform these difficult moves (*"la capriola le insegnerò,"* "I'll teach you to do the capriole"), with the implication that it will be against the count's wishes.

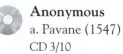

Anonymous
a. Pavane (1547)
CD 3/10

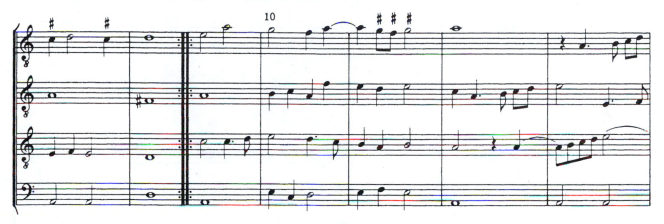

Anonymous
b. Galliard (1547)
Thomson-Schirmer Website

Renaissance Instruments and Instrumental Music

Chapter 23

62

Miguel de Fuenllana
Fantasia (1554)

The guitar heard in so much of today's popular music had its origins in late medieval Spain, where the instrument was called the *vihuela*. (To see an early guitar, or *vihuela*, turn to MWC, Fig. 23-4.) The *vihuela* was a four-, five-, or six-string instrument tuned, in many cases, exactly like the lute (in fourths, with a third in the middle). Beginning in the sixteenth century, Spanish composers in particular began to publish large collections of guitar music that included intabulations of vocal music, even polyphonic Masses and motets. They also included new compositions in the purely instrumental genres of prelude, ricercar, and fantasia. One such anthology of guitar music was Miguel de Fuenllana's *Orphenica lyra* (*Orpheus' Lyre*), a thousand copies of which were printed in Seville in 1554.

Fuenllana's Fantasia No. 9 is typical of the newly composed fantasias contained in *Orphenica lyra*. A fantasia is much like the ricercar of the period—a collection of imitative passages that unfolds rather freely. Fantasia No. 9 contains four separate imitative themes, or points of imitation, and these are worked out in succession (they enter in bars 1, 30, 55, and 82). Notice the somewhat carefree approach to the integrity of the counterpoint. Voices seem to enter and exit willy-nilly. Sometimes there are four, sometimes three, and sometimes only two (see mm. 22–36, for example). This is typical of guitar and lute music during the sixteenth and seventeenth centuries. When this discontinuous texture appears in the later Baroque period, it is called *stile brisé* (French for "broken style"; see MWC, Chapter 36). Finally, notice that Fuenllana's entire fantasia is in what we would call a minor key (really a doubly transposed Dorian mode). Yet the final triad includes a raised third producing what is now called a "Picardy" third. This practice of changing minor thirds to major in the final chord of a keyboard piece will become even more pronounced during the Baroque era, especially in the minor-key toccatas, fantasias, and fugues of J.S. Bach. Finally, this fantasia was notated in Spanish tablature, which uses a grid that places the highest-sounding pitches in the lowest lines visually.

Miguel de Fuenllana
Fantasia (1554)
Thomson-Schirmer Website

63

Claudio Merulo
Canzona 5 (c1600)

By the end of the Renaissance, composers were beginning to write music suitable for instruments, particularly wind instruments. During the seventeenth century, composers would continue to highlight the unique capabilities of the different instruments, and many more distinctly idiomatic styles would emerge as instrumental music gradually achieved parity with vocal music. Some of the first idiomatic writing for wind instruments is found in the canzona. This genre originated as an instrumental incarnation of the French chanson. When intended for wind ensemble, a canzona generally avoided fast scalar runs, which on some wind instruments were difficult to play in tune. Yet the instrumental canzona emphasized strong, clear-cut rhythms and frequent repeated pitches, which favored wind instruments like the sackbut and cornett, which can easily generate sharp attacks.

Venetian organist Claudio Merulo must have heard the wind ensemble employed by the Doge of Venice in his basilica of St. Mark on countless occasions. Presumably, it was for this Venetian ensemble that Merulo composed Canzona 5, the fifth in a set of canzonas that he wrote around 1600. Canzona 5 begins with sprightly imitation and proceeds to work through four additional points of imitation (which appear in bars 25, 37, 63, and 78). Only once does the imitation stop—at the striking chordal passage in measures 71–76. Toward the end (m. 86) the first imitative theme returns to round off this impressive work. This edition of Canzona 5 was especially prepared for this anthology by Michael Holmes of the Washington Cornett and Sackbutt Ensemble, as was the accompanying recording. On the recording, the upper two lines are played on cornett and the bottom two on sackbut. As the performers play the canzona, they ornament along the way and add their own *musica ficta*.

Claudio Merulo
Canzona 5 (c1600)
CD 3/11

Edited by Michael Holmes

Religious Music in Three German Cities
The Protestant-Catholic Confrontation

64

Heinrich Isaac
a. *Innsbruck, ich muss dich lassen* (c1510)
b. *Innsbruck, ich muss dich lassen* (c1515)

Innsbruck, Austria, is a beautiful Alpine city, and the site of the 1964 Winter Olympics. Today tourists walk around the charming central zone, visit the building where Emperor Maximilian died in 1519, and marvel at the statuary designed by Albrecht Dürer inside the Hofkapelle (court chapel), where Heinrich Isaac and the other members of the chapel sang. Accompanying visitors on their walk—piped in over a public address system—are the sounds of traditional Tyrolean music, including the famous *Innsbruck, ich muss dich lassen* (*Innsbruck, I must now leave you*). Likely this was a popular monophonic song before Isaac took up the tune early in the sixteenth century and dressed it in the finery of learned polyphony. In fact, Isaac did so twice, once in Tenorlied format, with the melody in the tenor voice (64a), and again, presumably later, with the tune in the soprano voice (64b). Of course, by repositioning the song, Isaac was obliged to rewrite the harmony supporting it. He took advantage of the opportunity to insert a rich E♭ chord in the midst of what is essentially an F harmony. Isaac also extended the second version by repeating the last four bars. Today the second setting is the better known of the two, and that is the version on our recording.

Innsbruck, ich muss dich lassen,	Innsbruck, I must now leave you
Ich fahr dahin mein Strassen,	I'm going on my way,
In fremde Land dahin.	Far in a foreign land.
Mein Freud ist mir genommen	My joy from me is taken,
Die ich nit weiss bekommen,	I know not how to get it back,
Wo ich im Elend bin.	While I travel in misery.

Heinrich Isaac

a. *Innsbruck, ich muss dich lassen* (c1510)

Heinrich Isaac
b. *Innsbruck, ich muss dich lassen* (c1515)
CD 3/12

65

Paul Hofhaimer
Salve, Regina for Organ (c1510?)

The *Salve, Regina* (*Hail, Queen*) was, and remains, one of the most beloved melodies in the repertoire of Gregorian chant. We encountered this chant before, in conjunction with Philippe Basiron's paraphrase motet (see *MWC*, p. 137, where the beginning of the *Salve, Regina* can be found before Basiron's motet). The plainsong *Salve, Regina* was created by an unknown author during the early thirteenth century, just after the years in which Leoninus and Perotinus composed their organum versions of *Viderunt omnes*. The chant *Salve, Regina* and three other important antiphons in honor of the Virgin Mary formed a collection of four important Marian antiphons. In many locations one of these four chants was sung, or occasionally played on an organ in alternation with singers, at the end of each day. The chant that was sung was determined by the particular moment in the liturgical year; the *Salve, Regina*, for example, was sung before retiring during the summer and fall months.

Like a religious folk song, the *Salve, Regina* sounded forth in every country around the Latin Christian world. Not surprisingly, however, just as there are regional differences in folk songs, so there were regional variants of this chant. In the setting for organ by Paul Hofhaimer, the chant stands like a cantus firmus in long notes in the tenor. Notice that the version sung in the German-speaking lands has an upper neighboring tone after the first note, unlike the versions sung in Italy and France (MWC, p. 137). The anthology gives only Hofhaimer's setting for the first phrase of the chant. The second phrase would be sung by the choir, the third played by the organ, the fourth by the choir, and so on in *alternatim* fashion. The organ on which this recording was made is at the cathedral of St. Valère in Sion, Switzerland, which dates from 1390 and is reputed to be the oldest organ surviving today in playable condition.

Paul Hofhaimer
Salve, Regina for Organ (c1510?)
CD 3/13

66

Martin Luther/Johann Walter

a. Martin Luther, *Ein feste Burg ist unser Gott*, Chorale (1529)

b. Johann Walter, *Ein feste Burg ist unser Gott*, 4-part setting (1529)

As we have seen, Martin Luther was a church reformer with a special love, and skill, for music. He played the flute and lute, and was said to have a fine, but soft, tenor voice. Music was, for Luther, "the excellent gift of God." Thus it is not surprising to learn that Luther himself composed the texts and melodies to at least sixteen Lutheran chorales as part of his effort to provide appropriate music for the services of his evangelical church. In addition, Luther produced nine other chorales simply by replacing the Latin text with a new German one, thereby creating in each case a contrafactum.

The chorale *Ein feste Burg ist unser Gott* (*A Mighty Fortress Is Our God*) is typical of those composed by Luther and of the German chorale in general. First of all, it is easy to sing, a distinct advantage for Lutheran congregations, who were asked to participate directly in the music of the service. The melody spans exactly an octave and emphasizes the strong scale degrees of the mode (here Lydian with B♭)—degrees 1, 5, and 8. As is also true for many chorales, *Ein feste Burg* unfolds in **AAB** form, perhaps because many secular German Lieder of this time and earlier had such a formal plan. Finally, both text and tune possess a certain militant tone, urging the Lutheran faithful to fight the good fight against the forces of evil. In Luther's mind, surely, "der alte böse Feind" ("the old wicked enemy") sat on the papal throne in Rome. *Ein feste Burg* remains to this day the signature melody of the Lutheran church, where it is sung annually on Reformation Sunday (31 October).

To supply the newly reformed church with more elaborate polyphony—and to have a repertory of learned music that might be taught in the schools—Luther collaborated with a musician more thoroughly trained in the art of counterpoint: Johann Walter. In 1524 Walter, with Luther's blessing, issued his hymnbook *Geistliche Gesangbüchlein* (*Little Book of Spiritual Songs*), setting the newly created chorales of Luther and others in three-, four-, and five-voice arrangements. (*Ein feste Burg* appeared in a subsequent edition of this popular collection, in 1529.) In these settings, Walter simply followed the model of Heinrich Isaac (no. 64) and other composers of polyphonic German Lieder. He placed the tune in the tenor, thereby creating a Tenorlied, and surrounded it with lightly imitative counterpoint.

Martin Luther

a. *Ein feste Burg ist unser Gott*, Chorale (1529)

CD 3/14

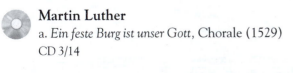

Ein fe-ste Burg ist un-ser Gott, ein gu-te Wehr und Waf-fen. Der al-te bö-se
Er hilft uns frei aus al-ler Not, die uns jetzt hat be-trof-fen.

Feind, mit Ernst er's jetzt meint, gross Macht und viel List sein grau-sam Rüst-ung ist, auf Erd' ist nichts seins Glei-chen.

Johann Walter

b. *Ein feste Burg ist unser Gott*, 4-part setting (1529)

CD 3/15

247

Ein feste Burg ist unser Gott,	A mighty fortress is our God,
Ein gute Wehr und Waffen.	A bulwark never failing.
Er hilft uns frei aus aller Not	Our helper he amid the flood
Die uns jetzt hat betroffen.	Our mortal ills prevailing.
Der alte böse Feind	For still our ancient foe
Mit Ernst er's jetzt meint,	Does seek to work us woe,
Gross Macht und viel List	His craft and power are great
Sein grausam Rüstung ist,	And armed with cruel hate,
Auf Erd' ist nicht seins Gleichen.	On earth is not his equal.

67

Orlande de Lassus
De profundis clamavi (c1560)

Orlande de Lassus was an enormously prolific and versatile composer who left us more than a thousand compositions. French chanson, German Lied, Italian madrigal, Mass, Magnificat, motet—he felt at home in each of these musical genres. Indeed, during the sixteenth century no other composer's music was so often and so widely published throughout Europe than his. Knighted by the pope, Lassus was known as the "prince of music."

In his own day, Lassus was particularly admired for his motets, owing to their technical perfection and expressive power. No collection of motets by Lassus is more demonstrative of his capacity for rhetorical persuasion than his seven Penitential Psalms. We have met the Penitential Psalms before, with the motet *Miserere mei, Deus* composed by Josquin des Prez (no. 59). Lassus was the first composer to set all seven of these remorseful texts as a single unit. The sixth in the set, Psalm 129, *De profundis clamavi* (*From the depths I cried to you*), expresses the anguish of the sinner who cries from the depths of the soul for divine forgiveness. The challenge for Lassus was both technical and expressive—to honor the ancient psalm tone, yet to do justice to the even more venerable Psalter of the Old Testament. The psalm tone (being essentially the reiteration of a reciting tone and cadence), is the musical equivalent of handcuffs. As you listen to this composition, follow the progress of the psalm tone as Lassus moves it from voice to voice in each successive verse. Despite the constriction of the psalm tone, Lassus creates settings of exceptional beauty. Perhaps most impressive is verse five, in which the tone is placed in the bass; this usually mobile voice is limited to stepwise motion, yet the harmony still sounds powerfully persuasive. Notice in particular that in verses two and three Lassus involves the psalm tone in two canons, the first with the tone upright, and the second with it turned upside down (in musical inversion). (Only the first six verses are heard on the recording, though all ten are provided in the score.)

Orlande de Lassus
De profundis clamavi (c1560)
CD 3/16

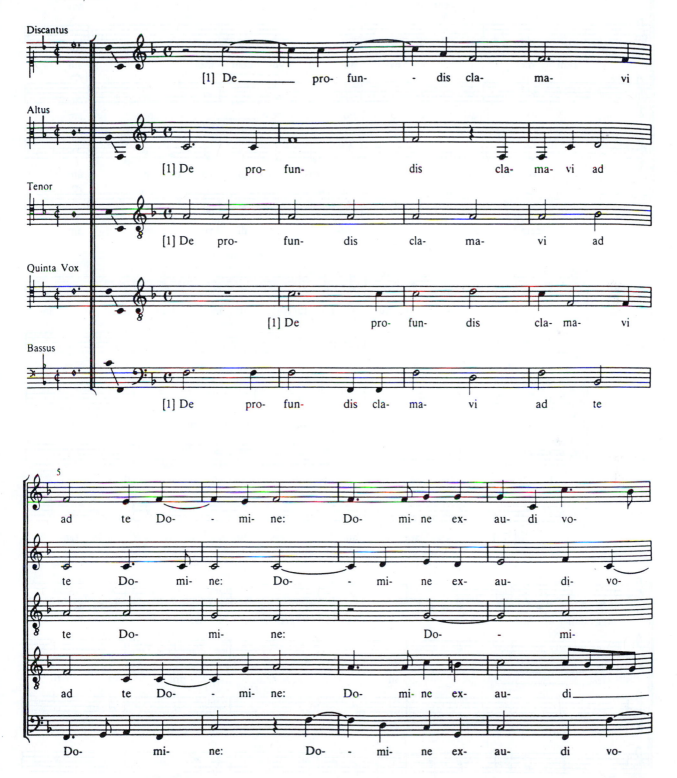

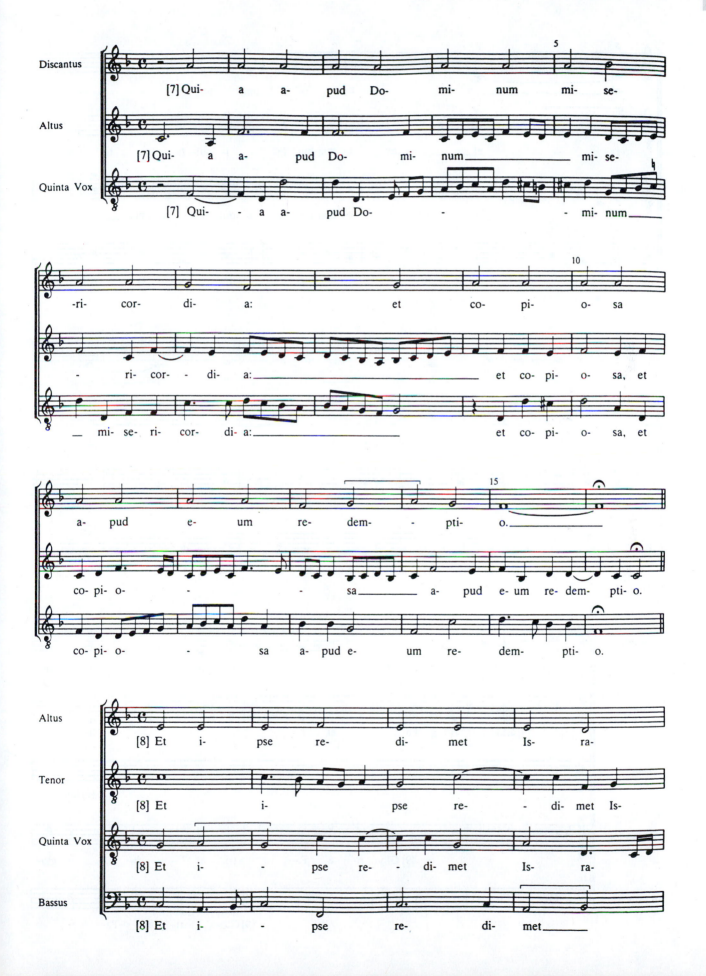

De profundis clamavi ad te Domine: Domine exaudi vocem meam.	From the depths I have cried to thee, O Lord: Lord, hear my voice.
Fiant aures tuae intendentes in vocem deprecationis meae.	Let thy ears be attentive to the voice of my supplication.
Si iniquitates observaveris Doimine: Domine, quis sustinebit?	If thou, O Lord, wilt mark iniquities: Lord, who shall stand?
Quia apud te propitiatio est: et propter legem tuam sustinui te Domine.	For with thee there is merciful forgiveness: and by reason of thy law, I have waited for thee, O Lord.
Sustinuit anima mea in verbo ejus: speravit anima mea in Domino.	My soul hath relied on his word: my soul hath hoped in the Lord.
A custodia matutina usque ad noctem, speret Israel in Domino.	From the morning watch even until night, let Israel hope in the Lord.
Quia apud Dominum misericordia: et copiosa apud eum redemptio.	Because with the Lord there is mercy: and with him plentiful redemption.
Et ipse redimet Israel ex omnibus iniquitatibus ejus.	And he shall redeem Israel from all his iniquities.
Gloria Patri, et Filio, et Spiritui Sancto. Sicut erat in principio, et nunc, et semper, et in saecula seculorum. Amen.	Glory be to the Father, and to the Son, and to the Holy Ghost. As it was in the beginning, is now and ever shall be, world without end. Amen.

Chapter 25

Rome and Music of the Counter-Reformation

68

Giovanni Pierluigi da Palestrina
Sanctus of the *Missa Aeterna Christi munera* (1590)

Of Palestrina's 104 Masses, only forty-three were published during his lifetime. While very few can be dated with any accuracy, the *Missa Aeterna Christi munera* was published in his *Missarum liber quintus* (*Fifth Book of Masses*, 1590) and is believed to have been composed sometime between 1580 and 1590. That decade had been an eventful one in Palestrina's life. After thirty-three years of marriage, his first wife died of the plague. He subsequently married a wealthy widow and spent his time working as choirmaster for the Capella Giulia in the Vatican, participating in his second wife's fur-trading business, speculating in Roman real estate, and composing masterpieces.

Palestrina's Masses vary from the six- and eight-part works for important feasts in the liturgical year to four-part compositions intended for ordinary usage. *Missa*

Aeterna Christi munera is in the latter category. This Mass is based on the hymn *Aeterna Christi munera*, which was sung on the Feast of the Martyrs and Apostles. Palestrina used each of the hymn's four phrases as a point of imitation. The opening phrase of the *Sanctus* illustrates some of the characteristics of Palestrina's imitative style. After singing the point of imitation, each voice continues to spin out new polyphony based on the shape of the chant. When the music arrives at the cadence in measure 13, the alto and tenor simultaneously begin the new phrase. This type of phrase elision allows for the necessary harmonic and melodic repose while maintaining the unbroken rhythmic pulsation of the polyphony. Careful placement of dissonance on points of weak rhythmic stress and the resolution of suspensions further this gentle pulsation. The result is a musical style that reflects the timeless and serene nature of devotion and worship that has made Palestrina's music so admired for centuries. The "Benedictus" and the final "Hosanna" are not included in the recording.

Giovanni Pierluigi da Palestrina
Sanctus of the *Missa Aeterna Christi munera* (1590)
CD 3/17

Sanctus

Benedictus

Hosanna

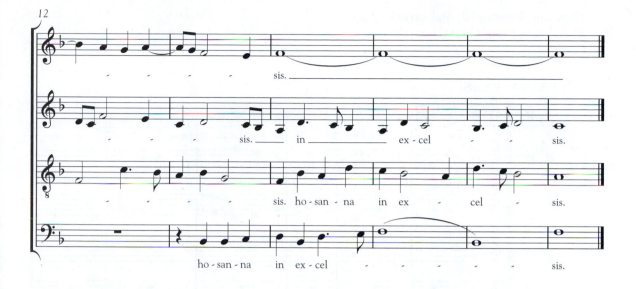

Sanctus, Sanctus, Sanctus	Holy, Holy, Holy
Dominus Deus Sabaoth.	Lord God almighty.
Pleni sunt coeli et terra gloria tua.	Heaven and earth are filled with your glory.
Hosanna in excelsis.	Hosanna in the highest.
Benedictus qui venit in nomine Domini.	Blessed is he that comes in the name of the Lord.
Hosanna in excelsis.	Hosanna in the highest.

69

Giovanni Pierluigi da Palestrina
Motet: *Tu es Petrus* (1573)
(Prima pars)

This six-part motet illustrates the skillful manner in which Palestrina manipulates musical texture, creating variety with only six lines of polyphony. The opening measures contrast trios of high and low voices, and the phrase ends by expanding the texture to a quartet. The four-part texture continues for the next section (beginning in m. 15), but when the second quartet (mm. 20–24) repeats the phrase "aedificabo ecclesiam meam," it inverts the counterpoint of the previous phrase, giving a new twist to the same musical material (see chart). From measure 25 to the cadence in measure 32, the polyphony expands to simultaneously include all six voices for the first time. This pattern of changing voice combinations and alternations between homophonic and polyphonic passages continues for the remainder of the motet.

phrase	mm. 15–19	mm. 20–24
a	Soprano I	Alto
b	Alto	Tenor
c	Tenor	Soprano II
d	Bass	Baritone

Giovanni Pierluigi da Palestrina
Motet: *Tu es Petrus* (1573)
CD 3/18

Tu es Petrus,
et super hanc petram edificabo ecclesiam
    meam,
et portae interi non praevalebunt adversus
    eam.
Et tibi dabo claves regni coelorum.

You are Peter,
and upon this rock I will build my
    church,
and the gates of hell shall not prevail
    against it.
And I will give to you the keys of the
    kingdom of heaven.

70

Giovanni Pierluigi da Palestrina
Kyrie of the *Missa Tu es Petrus* (c1585)

Palestrina treats this parody or emulation of his own motet with great flexibility. The first "Kyrie" section is based on the beginning phrase of the motet, but with some significant changes. Instead of opening with a high trio of voices, as in the motet, the Mass begins with roughly the same material but now in the lower three voices. After the initial statement, the remainder of the section is a free development of prominent motives from all three parts of the motet phrase, especially the eighth-note figure drawn from the lowest of the trio voices. One minor change from the motet is that the rhythm of the music is altered to fit the "Kyrie" text. The "Christe" section also freely develops motives, but from the "aedificabo ecclesiam meam" section of the motet. Notice in particular how the Soprano I and II of the "Christe" conflate the Soprano I and Tenor from measures 15–16 in the motet. The final "Kyrie" begins with a free development of motives derived from the motet, but for the final bars (mm. 80–88) it returns to a loose imitation of the motet's final phrase ("claves regni coelorum"; m. 78 to the end). The numerous voice crossings, especially between the two soprano parts, lend a lightness and grace to the polyphony.

Giovanni Pierluigi da Palestrina
Kyrie of the *Missa Tu es Petrus* (c1585)
CD 3/19

276

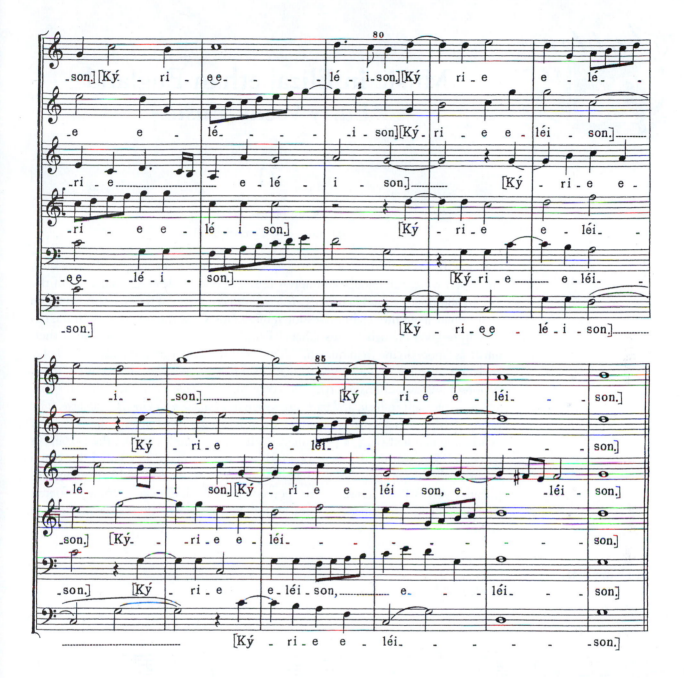

Kyrie eleison.
Christe eleison.
Kyrie eleison.

Lord, have mercy upon me.
Christ, have mercy upon me.
Lord, have mercy upon me.

Chapter 26

Music in Elizabethan England
Early Vocal Music

71

King Henry VIII
Pastyme with Good Companye (c1520)

Henry VIII was well educated in languages, mathematics, theology, and astronomy, and could write well enough to impress Erasmus, one the leading humanists of the day. In addition, he was handsome, athletic, and an excellent musician. As king, he maintained about fifty-eight professional musicians. Only the best singers in the nation were good enough for his Chapel Royal. One Italian visitor described their music as "more divine than human." Henry VIII was also a good lutenist, could play keyboard instruments, and loved to sight-read part songs with competent courtiers. Among his compositions are two five-voice Masses, some instrumental works that are quite pleasant to hear, and part songs such as *Pastyme with Good Companye*. The lilting rhythm and simple, joyous melody of this song have worn well, even after nearly five hundred years of performances. It is not complex music; the two upper parts each keep within the range of a fifth and often proceed in parallel thirds and sixths while the bass provides the harmonic foundation. Its form is likewise uncomplicated: **AA'BB'**. This is music for boon companions sharing an evening of friendship and liquid refreshment, not for professional musicians singing before a royal audience.

King Henry VIII
Pastyme with Good Companye (c1520)
CD 3/20

1.

Pastyme with good companye,
I love and shall unto I die;
Gruch so will but none deny,
So God be pleas'd, so live will I;
For my pastance,
Hunt, sing and dance,
My heart is set,
To my comfort,
All goodly sport:
Who shall me let?

2.

Youth must have some dalliance,
Of good or ill some pastance;
Company methinks then best
All thoughts and fancies to digest,
For idleness
Is chief mistress
Of vices all:
Then who can say
But mirth and play
Is best of all?

3.

Company with honesty
Is virtue, vices to flee;
Company is good and ill,
But every man hath his free will.
The best ensue,
The worst eschew,
My mind shall be;
Virtue to use,
Vice to refuse,
Thus shall I use me.

72

Thomas Tallis
Psalm 2 (1567)
(Psalm 2: *Why fum'th in sight*)

Thomas Tallis was the leading English composer of the generation that preceded William Byrd, and the sovereigns of England so valued his talent that whether Catholic or Protestant, they provided him with court patronage and protection from religious persecution. His music ranges from deceptively simple psalm tunes and the anthem *If ye love me* to elaborate motets such as *Spem in alium*, his famous work that calls for forty different voice parts.

Tallis composed eight tunes for the metrical Psalter published in 1567 by Elizabeth's Archbishop of Canterbury, Matthew Parker, and intended for congregational use and private devotion. Parker's version not only recasts the biblical prose into poetic meter, but also interprets the Old Testament in light of Christian theology. Because Parker arranged all his psalm translations into a few standard poetic meters, Tallis did not need to compose a separate tune for each of the 150 psalms. Nearly all the psalms could be sung to one of his eight tunes. The free alternation between what we would call E-major and E-minor chords in this third-mode (Phrygian) tune is one of its most attractive features. Centuries later, Ralph Vaughan Williams high-lighted this harmonic contrast in his *Fantasy on a Theme of Thomas Tallis* (1910).

Thomas Tallis
Psalm 2
Thomson-Schirmer Website

**Parker's metrical translation,
set by Tallis**

Why fum'th in sight the Gentils spite,
In fury raging stout?
Why taketh in bond[1] the people fond,
vaine thinges to bring about?
The kinges arise, the lordes devise,
in counsayles mett therto,
Agaynst the Lord: with false accord,
against his Christ they go.

Let us they say: break downe their ray[2]
of all their bondes and cordes:
We will renounce: that they pronounce,
their loores[3] as stately lordes.
But God of might: in heaven so bright,
Shall laugh them all to scorne:
The Lord on hie: shall them defie,
they shall be once forlorne.

Then shall his ire: speake all in fire,
to them agayne therfore:
He shall with threate: their malice beate,
in his displeasure sore.
Yet am I set: a king so great,
on Sion hill full fair:
Though me they kill: yet will that hill,
my lawe and worde outcast.

Gods wordes decreed: I (Christ)[4] wil sprede
for God thus sayd to mee:
My sonne I say: thou art, this day,
I have begotten thee.
Aske thou of mee: I will geve thee,
to rule all Gentils landes:
Thou shalt possesse: in faernesse[5],
the world how wide it standes.

With iron rod: as mighty God,
all rebels shalt thou bruse:
And breake them all: in pieces small,
as sherdes[6] the potters use.
Be wise therefore: ye kinges the more,
Receyve ye wisdomes lore:
Ye judges strong: of right and wrong,
advise you now before.

**The Bishop's Bible (1568)
Psalm 2 (spelling modernized)**

1. Why do the heathen so furiously rage together: and why do the people imagine a vain thing?

2. The kings of the earth stand by, and the rulers take counsel together: against the Lord, and against his anointed.

3. Let us break their bonds asunder: and cast away their cords from us.

4. He that dwelleth in heaven shall laugh them to scorn: the Lord shall have them in derision.

5. Then shall he speak unto them in his wrath: and vex them in his sore displeasure.

6. Yet have I set my king: upon my holy hill of Zion.

7. I will preach the law, whereof the Lord hath said unto me: thou art my son, this day have I begotten thee.

8. Desire of me, and I shall give thee, the heathen for thine inheritance: and the uttermost parts of the earth for thy possession.

9. Thou shalt bruise them with a rod of iron: and break them in pieces like a potter's vessel.

10. Be wise now therefore, O ye kings: be learned ye that are judges of the earth.

[1] Shortened form of "bondage," as in "Why do the people so willingly place themselves in bondage to vain things?" This verse appears twice in Parker's Psalter, and uses a different word in each instance. In the psalter, the word is "bond," but in the text underlay for Psalm Tune 3, the word has been changed to "hand." While the meaning of bond is not as clear as hand, it fits to the rhyme pattern better.
[2] Shortened form of array, especially of soldiers, as in battle-ray.
[3] "Lures," as in "We will renounce the lures (temptations) offered by the wicked."
[4] Inserted by Archbishop Parker
[5] Fairness
[6] Shards

The Lorde in feare: your service beare,
with dread to him rejoyce:
Let rages be: resist not ye,
him serve with joyfull voyce.
The sonne kisse ye: less wroth he be,
lose not the way of rest:
For when his ire: is set on fire,
who trust in hym be blest.

11. Serve the Lord in fear: and rejoice unto him
with reverence.

12. Kiss the son, lest he be angry, and so ye
perish from the right way: if his wrath be
kindled (yea but a little) blessed are all they
that put their trust in him.

73

William Byrd
O Lord, make thy servant, Elizabeth (c1570)

The reign of Elizabeth I finally brought a measure of religious stability to England. After the brief return of Catholicism under her elder half-sister, Queen Mary (whose nickname "Bloody Mary" resulted from her burning Protestants at the stake), the Anglican Church was firmly established. Elizabeth may have been Protestant, but her services were so full of religious ritual and ceremony that Catholic visitors from foreign courts thought the only significant difference from Rome was the language. While musicians were not patronized with the same lavish expenditures as had occurred under Henry VIII, those who were named "Gentlemen in ordinary" of the Chapel Royal were fortunate. They received twice the salary of other church musicians in the realm, could supplement their income by singing elsewhere, and had approximately one hundred days per year in which their services were not required.

The anthem O Lord, make thy servant, Elizabeth is representative of the type of music performed in the Chapel Royal and at other cathedrals throughout England. Numerous versions of this anthem exist, often with the name of one of the two following kings, James I and Charles I, inserted in place of Elizabeth. The anthem's text is based on Psalm 21:2 and 4, so the composition also divides into two sections, one for each verse, and concludes with a beautiful Amen. While there are numerous cadences within each section, they are elided with the opening of new phrases. The text painting that is so characteristic of the Elizabethan English madrigal is completely absent here; however, even with dense imitative polyphony, the text is clear and easily understood. In this edition, the anthem has been transposed up a minor third to make it easier to sing.

William Byrd
O Lord, make thy servant, Elizabeth (c1570)
CD 3/21

IV-V 14.2-15.2: unison tenors sing different words in all sources.

25: *prevent*: predispose to repentance and faith.

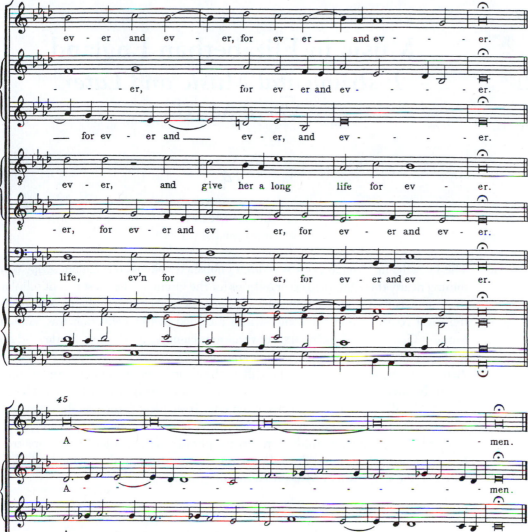

Chapter 27

Music in Elizabethan England
Instrumental Music and Later Vocal Music

74

Thomas Morley
Goe from my window (c1590)

The Fitzwilliam Virginal Book was not a published volume, but a manuscript containing nearly three hundred compositions for the virginal. The most recent scholarship suggests that it was compiled by a number of scribes who probably worked for the royal court. One of the compositions included in this collection was Thomas Morley's *Goe from my window*, a set of variations based on a folk song. Morley did not begin his set of variations with a simple statement of the theme, but launched immediately into the first variation and withheld the clearest statement of the theme until the fifth variation (variation 5). The theme itself consists of four two-bar phrases (**ABB'A'**), all of which are variants of the same basic idea. Surprising shifts between major and minor chords (such as A major and A minor in mm. 3–6) provide a measure of harmonic interest to these repetitive phrases. The first four variations treat the theme with the greatest flexibility, while the last three pit the theme (or its harmony, in the sixth variation) against a running countermelody.

Thomas Morley
Goe from my window (c1590)
CD 3/22

6.

7.

75

Thomas Weelkes

As Vesta Was from Latmos Hill Descending (1601)

This composition is one of twenty-five madrigals that Thomas Morley gathered into a collection honoring Queen Elizabeth I, entitled *The Triumphes of Oriana*. Morley based his idea on a recent Italian collection of madrigals that had been published in 1592 by a wealthy Venetian, who had hired poets and composers to provide text and music in honor of his wife. The Venetian's only stipulation was that each madrigal had to conclude with the phrase "Long live the beautiful Dori," the mythological name given to his wife. Morley shamelessly adopted not only the title (*Il Trionfo di Dori*), but also the idea. He asked for contributions from English poets and musicians—some so obscure that their only published work is in this collection. Like the model, all the madrigals are unified with the closing phrase "Long live fair Oriana." Weelkes, who was one of the most skilled of the contributors, wrote a six-part work that is filled with obvious madrigalisms: "running down" is set to a rapidly descending scale, and a trio sings "three by three." The composition has a musical architecture that can be described as **ABCDCBA**, a form that is based not on musical themes but on contrasts of texture.

Thomas Weelkes
As Vesta Was from Latmos Hill Descending (1601)
CD 3/23

76

John Dowland
Flow my tears (1600)

It seems that John Dowland considered his life a sad journey through a vale of tears. As an adult he signed his name "John Dowland de Lachrimae" ("John Dowland of the tears") and entitled one of his lute compositions "Semper Dowland semper dolens" ("Always Dowland, always doleful"), a pun that suggests how he pronounced his name (as in "Doeland"). He experienced great success abroad, where he was the highest-paid musician in the court of King Christian IV of Denmark; yet for many years his attempts to receive a court appointment in England went unfulfilled. In 1600 Dowland published his *Second Book of Songs or Ayres*. The second work in the collection was *Flow my tears*. This song is based on his lute pavane, *Lachrime* (c1595), and the fact that the text fits the preexistent phrases of the pavane so closely suggests that Dowland was probably the author of the heartfelt poem. The most characteristic musical gesture in this ayre is the descending tetrachord. Numerous phrases encompass a descending fourth—there are two descending minor tetrachords within the first measure alone. Dowland concludes the song with another group of fourths, this time to the text "Happy, happy" (m. 19). However, we soon realize it is not that the singer is happy, but that he believes the inhabitants of hell are happy in comparison. The form of *Flow my tears* is **AABBCC**, and unlike many of Dowland's songs, it is through-composed instead of strophic. The final phrases of **A** and **C** are tied together by means of a musical rhyme.

John Dowland
Flow my tears (1600)
CD 3/24

night's black   bird   her   sad in - fa - my sings,   There   let me   live   for -
in   de - spair   their   last   for - tunes de - plore,   Light   doth but shame   dis -

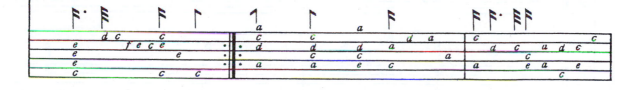

- lorn.   Nev - er may my woes   be re - liev - ed,   Since pi -
- close.   From the high - est spire   of con - tent - ment,   My for -

- ty   is fled,   And tears,   and sighs,   and groans   my wea - ry
- tune is thrown,   And fear,   and grief,   and pain   for my de -

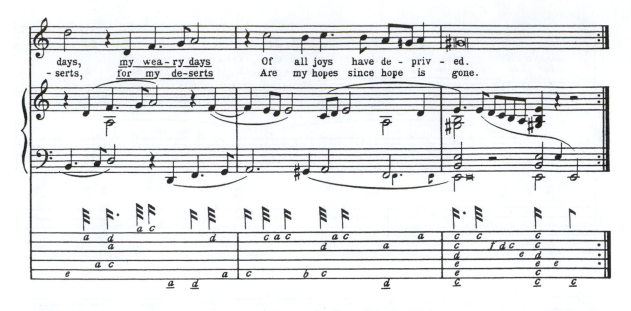

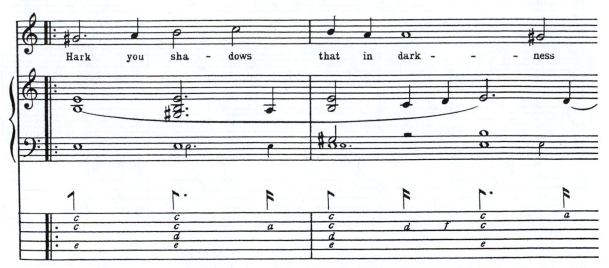

that in hell Feel not the world's de - - - spite.

The Later Madrigal in Ferrara and Mantua
Gesualdo and Monteverdi

Chapter 28

77

Carlo Gesualdo
Moro, lasso (1613)

Gesualdo's music sounds so strikingly dissonant that one might easily wonder what type of seventeenth-century audience would listen to it, much less purchase books of his madrigals. In fact, his music was highly esteemed by aristocratic amateurs and connoisseurs. Queen Christina of Sweden and Cardinal Francesco Barbarini, both of whom resided in Rome and supported sizable musical establishments, possessed copies of Gesualdo's madrigals. The queen even considered Gesualdo her favorite composer. Others have been fascinated as well. Igor Stravinsky once wrote: "Musicians may yet save Gesualdo from musicologists," meaning that this music is not merely a historical curiosity, but has its own artistic merit and relevance.[1] Not all Gesualdo's compositions share the "chromatic ecstasies" of *Moro, lasso*, but his music does demonstrate the most extreme example of the exaggerated interpretations madrigal composers used to set their texts. Certainly the opening chords have the

---

[1] Igor Stravinsky, Preface to *Gesualdo: The Man and His Music*, by Glenn Watkins (Chapel Hill, NC: University of North Carolina Press, 1973), v.

pungent dissonance that one eighteenth-century writer called "harsh, crude, and licentious modulation[s]," but the measures that immediately follow are routinely diatonic. It is this very diatonic normalcy that makes the startling dissonance possible. It is easy for modern listeners to focus on the harmony from a purely musical standpoint, but for Gesualdo, harmony was the maidservant of the text, and it is this textual relevance that made his music so admired by his (in a literal sense) peers.

Carlo Gesualdo
Moro, lasso (1613)
CD 3/25

Moro, lasso, al mio duolo
E chi mi può dar vita
Ahi, che m'ancide e non vuol darmi aita!
O dolorosa sorte,
Chi dar vita mi può, ahi, mi dà morte.

I die, miserable in my despair
And the one who can give me life
Ouch, that one kills me and gives no aid!
Oh, dolorous fate
The one who can give me life, alas, gives only
   death.

78

Claudio Monteverdi
Cruda Amarilli (1598, published 1605)

On 16 November 1598, Giovanni Maria Artusi (c1540–1613) accepted an impromptu invitation to hear some new, unpublished madrigals. Artusi was not some amateur curmudgeon who only liked the "tried and true." He had studied composition with Zarlino, the most important teacher of the period, and went to the performance eager to hear the "novelty" of these new works. However, he was deeply disturbed by Monteverdi's setting of *Cruda Amarilli* and wrote an open letter attacking the harsh, *unprepared* dissonances that were so foreign to the natural rules of harmony (see MWC, p. 229–230 for his specific criticisms). Monteverdi felt obliged to reply, and the result was a reasoned defense of the new Baroque aesthetic: that music was a means to an end (rather than art for art's sake). According to this philosophy, unusual form, harmony, and melody in the service of expression is no vice. Yet when compared with the music of Gesualdo, Monteverdi's harmony sounds pretty tame. (One wonders if the Prince of Venosa was shielded from Artusi's criticism by aristocratic privilege.) Unlike Gesualdo, who frequently juxtaposes unrelated chords in a slow, methodical manner, Monteverdi's dissonances are softened by the smooth and logical voice leading of the polyphony. Dissonance is often placed in weak rhythmic positions and leads to consonance. However, Monteverdi did not rely solely upon harmony to convey the text. Some of the most recognizable instances of madrigalisms occur with the phrases "ahi lasso" ("Ouch alas") and "e più fugace" ("yet more fleeting"), and the composition's conclusion is almost ironic, with "I mi morrò tacendo" ("I die in silence") repeated over and over and over again.

Cruda Amarilli che col nome ancora	Cruel Amarillys, who even through your name
D'amar ahi lasso! amaramente insegni.	Ouch alas! teach to love bitterly.
Amarilli del candido ligustro,	Amaryllis, more than the white privet
Più candida e più bella,	Pure and more beautiful
Ma dell'Aspido sordo	But more deaf than the wasp
E più sorda e più fera e più fugace.	And more fierce yet more fleeting
Poi che col dir t'offendo	Since in revealing I offend you
I mi morrò tacendo.	I will die silently.

Claudio Monteverdi
Cruda Amarilli (1598, published 1605)
CD 3/26

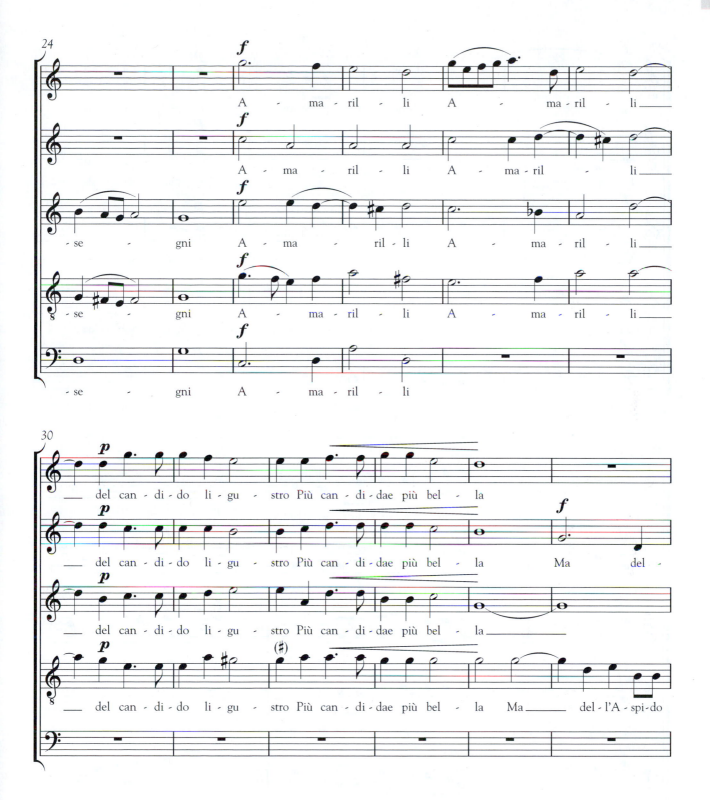

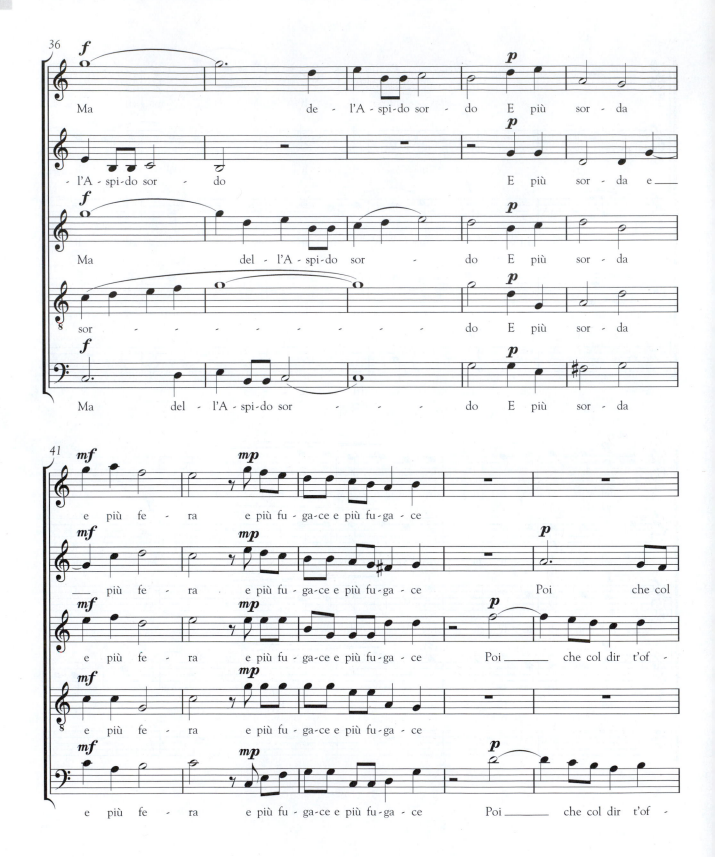

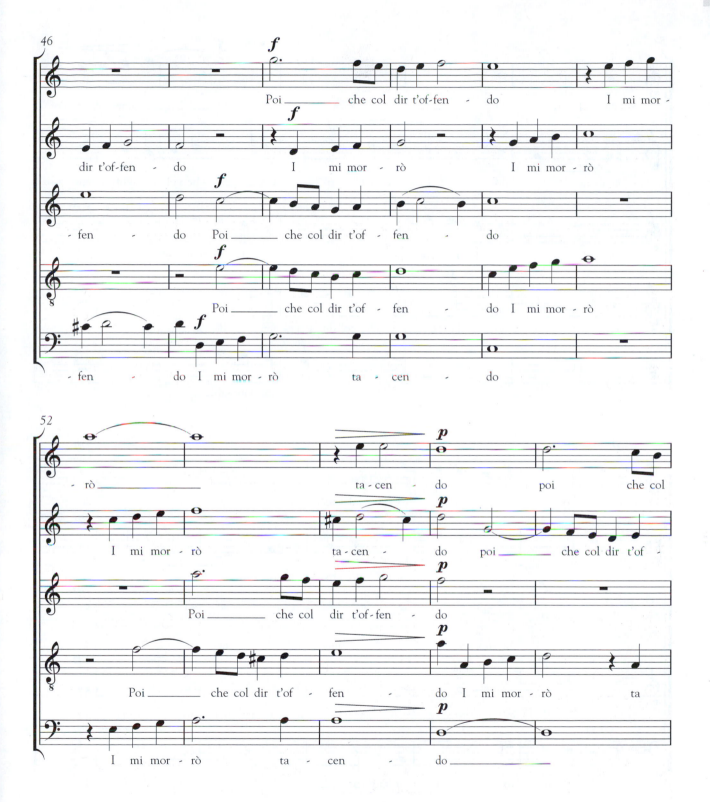